U0858375

毕节概览2022

OVERVIEW OF BIJIE 2022

中共毕节市委宣传部 编

贵州出版集团
贵州民族出版社

图书在版编目(CIP)数据

毕节概览. 2022 : 汉文、英文 / 中共毕节市委宣传部编. -- 贵阳 : 贵州民族出版社, 2023.9
ISBN 978-7-5412-2785-1

Ⅰ. ①毕… Ⅱ. ①中… Ⅲ. ①毕节－概况－2022－汉、英 Ⅳ. ①K927.33

中国国家版本馆CIP数据核字(2023)第070451号

毕节概览 2022
BIJIE GAILAN 2022

中共毕节市委宣传部　编

图片提供：中共毕节市委宣传部　贵州新闻图片社
出版发行：贵州民族出版社
地　　址：贵州省贵阳市观山湖区会展东路贵州出版集团大楼
邮　　编：550081
印　　刷：贵阳精彩数字印刷有限公司
版　　次：2023年9月第1版
印　　次：2023年9月第1次印刷
开　　本：889 mm×1194 mm　1/32
印　　张：4.5
字　　数：120千字
书　　号：ISBN 978-7-5412-2785-1
定　　价：98.00元

目　录

目录
Contents

毕节概览

2022

01

基本市情

Introduction to Bijie City

历史沿革 History

“毕节”一词作为国家行政管理的地名，目前可查的最早记录为《大定府志》卷之十一《沿革表第二》之夹注：“平夷去南秦近，且可控制建宁等郡，惟今毕节足以当之。毕节盖又平迟之转。夷书谓毕节为比跻之讹，比跻是其部人之名。方志谓毕节筑城以十二月晦始成，固名毕节。”

The name "Bijie" has a historical origin dating back to the earliest recorded instance in Volume 11 of *Dading Prefecture Annals*, specifically in the note for "*Table 2 for Historical Evolution*". It states that "Pingyi", a town close to Nanqin, controlled Jianning and adjacent counties. However, "Bijie" was deemed suitable to take Pingyi's place. It's believed that the name "Bijie" might have been derived from modifying "Pingchi". According to the books on the ethnic groups, originally the word Bijie refered to the local people. Later it was tranformed into another word which has the same sound

织金县平远古镇 Pingyuan Ancient Town, Zhijin County

大方县奢香古镇 Shexiang Ancient Town, Dafang County

of Bijie. However, the local record has another explaination that the place was named as Bijie because the construction of the city was completed on the last day of December. Bijie then implies that " A day for completion".

据考证，元初，平迟安德长官司于倒天河畔修建毕节驿；明洪武十六年（1383 年），置毕节卫，修毕节卫城。清康熙二十六年（1687 年），撤毕节卫、赤水卫建毕节县。民国沿用毕节县。中华人民共和国成立后，设贵州省人民政府毕节区行政督察专员公署。1970 年，毕节专区改为毕节地区。1994 年，撤毕节县设县级毕节市。2011 年，撤毕节地区设地级毕节市。

According to the historical records, the local official of Pingchi and Ande erected the posthouse along the banks of the Daotianhe River at the beginning of the Yuan Dynasty. Subsequently, in the 16th year of Hongwu's reign in the Ming Dynasty (1383 AD), Bijie Garrison was established, and the Bijie Garrison City was built. In the 26th year of Emperor Kangxi's reign of the Qing Dynasty (1687 AD),

Bijie Garrison and Chishui Garrison were dissolved and Bijie County was established. The name "Bijie County" continued to be used in the Republic of China. After the People's Republic of China was founded, the Bijie District Administrative Inspectorate Office of Guizhou Province was established. In 1970, Bijie Special District was renamed to Bijie District. In 1994, Bijie County was abolished and replaced by Bijie City at the county level. In 2011, Bijie District was abolished and replaced by Bijie City at the municipal level.

行政区划 Administrative Divisions

毕节市现辖区总面积2.69万平方千米。辖七星关区、大方县、黔西市、金沙县、织金县、纳雍县、威宁彝族回族苗族自治县、

毕节城区俯瞰图 Aerial view of Bijie urban area

赫章县 8 个县（自治县、市、区）和百里杜鹃管理区管理委员会 1 个正县级管委会。乡（镇、街道）279 个，其中街道 53 个，镇 135 个，非民族乡 19 个，民族乡 72 个；村（居）3,716 个，其中社区居民委员会 1,053 个，村民委员会 2,663 个。

The total area under the jurisdiction of Bijie City is 26,900 square kilometers, covering 8 counties and districts, namely Qixingguan District, Dafang County, Qianxi City, Jinsha County, Zhijin County, Nayong County, Weining Yi, Hui and Miao Autonomous County, Hezhang County. Additionally, there is one county-level management committee called Baili Dujuan Management Committee. In total, there are 279 townships (towns, sub-districts), including 53 sub-districts, 135 towns, 19 townships, and other 72 autonomous township of the ethnic minorities. There are 3,716 residential units in total, including 1,053 communities committe and 2,663 villagers'committee.

人口民族 Population and Ethnicity

截至2022年末，毕节市户籍人口950.05万人，常住人口681.59万人，境内居住着汉、彝、苗、回、布依等46个民族，少数民族人口占全市总人口的22.1%。人口超过万人的少数民族有：彝族75.38万人、苗族70.99万人、白族18.4万人、回族14万人、布依族9.96万人、仡佬族3.98万人、蒙古族3.92万人、满族1.27万人。

By the end of 2022, the household registered population of Bijie City was 9.5005 million among which 6.8159 million were permanent residents. The city is home to 46 ethnic groups, including Han, Yi, Miao, Hui, and Buyi. The ethnic minority groups account for 22.1% of the total population. Among them are the following groups whose

阿弓镇苗族同胞 The Miao girls in Agong Town

黔西市新仁苗族乡化屋村苗族同胞在围着篝火跳舞
The Miao dancing around a campfire in Huawu Village, Xinren Miao Township, Qianxi City

population exceeds 10,000: Yi (753,800), Miao (709,900), Bai (184,000), Hui (140,000), Buyi (99,600), Gelao (39,800), Mongolian (39,200), and Manchu (12,700).

区位气候 Climate

毕节市属亚热带湿润季风气候。四季分明，雨热同季，冬无严寒，夏无酷暑，气候类型多样，垂直（立体）气候特征明显，风能、太阳能资源丰富。年平均气温 13.6℃，年降水量 1,034.1 毫米，年平均日照时数 1,220.3 小时。秋冬季受冷空气和滇黔准静止锋影响，位于暖区一侧的区域风和日丽，位于冷区一侧的区域常出现连绵的阴雨天气；夏季除赤水河谷局地偶尔出现高温天气外，全市气候舒适，中高海拔地区冷凉及避暑气候特征明显。

织金县风光 Scenery of Zhijin County

Bijie City belongs to a subtropical humid monsoon climate. There are four distinct seasons with rain and heat in the same season, but there is no severe cold in winter, nor severe heat in summer. The climate in this city is multifaceted, with pronounced vertical (three-dimensional) climatic features and plentiful wind and solar resources. The city has an average annual temperature of 13.6℃ , an annual rainfall of 1,034.1 millimeters, and an average of 1220.3 hours of sunshine

per year. Affected by the cold air and the Yunnan-Guizhou quasi-stationary front in both autumn and winter, the warm area is sunny, whereas the cold area often has continuous cloudy and rainy weather. Generally speaking, the climate is comfortable, with evident coolness and summer resort characteristics in the mid-high altitude areas.

地形地貌 Topography

毕节市位于贵州省西北部，东经103°36′—106°44′，北纬26°21′—27°47′之间。东邻遵义市、贵阳市，南抵安顺市和六盘水市，西与云南省交界，北和四川省接壤。

Bijie City is located in the northwest of Guizhou Province, between 103°36′—106°44′ east longitude and 26°21′—27°47′ north latitude. It borders Zunyi City and Guiyang City in the east, Anshun City and Liupanshui City in the south, Yunnan Province in the west, and Sichuan Province in the north.

全市地处滇东高原向黔中山原过渡的斜坡地面，境内地势西高东低，呈阶梯状下降。地貌西部为高原、高山；中部为高中山、中山；东部为中山、低中山丘陵。境内最高点在赫章县南部珠市

织金大峡谷 Zhijin Grand Canyon

牛栏江大峡谷 Niulanjiang Grand Canyon

彝族乡韭菜坪，海拔 2,901 米，是全省最高峰；最低点在金沙县西北部，清池镇鱼塘河与赤水河汇合处，海拔 457 米，平均海拔 1,689 米。

The whole city is located on the slope of the transition from the eastern Yunnan plateau to the central Guizhou. The terrain is high in the west and low in the east, with a stepwise descent. There are plateaus and high mountains in the west, high-middle and middle mountains in the center, middle and low-middle mountains in the east. The highest point in the city is Jiucaiping, in Zhushi Yi Township, southern Hezhang County, with an altitude of 2,901 meters, making it the highest peak in the province. The lowest point is located at the confluence of Yutang River and Chishui River in Qingchi Town, northwest Jinsha County, with an altitude of 457 meters. The averaging altitude of Bijie city is 1,689 meters.

毕节概览

2022

02

自然资源

Natural Resources

矿产能源 Minerals

全市已发现矿产 60 余种，查明资源储量且具有开采价值的有 42 种。煤、铁、铜、铅、锌、稀土、钴、银矿保有资源量位列全省第一，钼、镍、硫铁、磷矿保有资源量位列全省第二。

More than 60 types of minerals have been discovered in the region, among which 42 types have proven to be resource reserves with mining value. The reserves, say coal, iron, copper, lead, zinc, rare earth, cobalt and silver, rank first, while the preserved resources of molybdenum, nickel, sulfur iron and phosphate rock rank second in Guizhou.

煤炭保有资源储量 325.53 亿吨，全省占比 40.69%；铁矿保有资源量 7.53 亿吨（矿石量），占全省保有资源量的 60.26%；铜矿保有资源量 11.53 万吨（金属量），占全省保有资源量的 69.21%；铅矿保有资源量 165.4 万吨（金属量），占全省保有资源量的 62.21%；锌矿保有资源量 379.1 万吨（金属量），占全省保有资源量的40.57%；稀土保有资源量 108.93 万吨（稀土氧化物），占全省保有资源量的 100%；钴矿保有资源量 89 吨（金属量），占全省保有资源量的 100%；银矿保有资源量 1,014.53 吨（金属量），占全省保有资源量的 72.06%；镍矿保有资源量 29.05 万吨（矿石量），占全省保有资源量的 45.76%；钼矿保有资源量 30.1 万吨

煤块 Coal block

（矿石量），占全省保有资源量的33.39%；硫铁矿保有资源量2.7亿吨（矿石量），占全省保有资源量的26.97%；磷矿保有资源量17.09亿吨，占全省保有资源量的34.91%。

铜 Copper

The coal reserve is 32.553 billion tons, accounting for 40.69% of the province; the iron mine has reserves of 0.753 billion tons (ore quantity), accounting for 60.26% of the total reserves; the copper mine has reserves of 0.1153 million tons (metal quantity), accounting for 69.21% of the total reserves in the province; the lead mine has reserves of 1.654 million tons (metal quantity), accounting for 62.21% of the total reserves in the province; the zinc mine has reserves of 3.791 million tons (metal quantity), accounting for 40.57% of the total reserves in the province; the rare earth mine has reserves of 1.0893 million tons (rare earth oxide), accounting for 100% of the total reserves in the province; the cobalt mine has reserves of 89 tons (metal quantity), accounting for 100% of the total reserves in the province; the silver mine has reserves of 1,014.53 tons (metal quantity), accounting for 72.06% of the total reserves in the province; the nickel mine has reserves of 0.2905 million tons (ore quantity), accounting for 45.76% of the total reserves in the province; the molybdenum mine has reserves of 0.301 million tons (ore quantity), accounting for 33.39% of the total reserves in the province; the pyrite mine has reserves of 0.27 billion tons (ore quantity), accounting for 26.97% of the total reserves in the province; the phosphate mine has reserves of 1.709 billion tons, accounting for 34.91% of the total reserves in the province.

生物资源 Biological Resources

动物资源：已查明的野生动物有 4 纲 29 目 278 种。其中两栖类动物 17 种，爬行类动物 28 种，鸟类 174 种，哺乳类动物 59 种。

The wild animals that have been identified in Bijie are categorized into 4 phyla, 29 orders, and 278 species. Of these, there are 17 species of amphibians, 28 species of reptiles, 174 species of birds, and 59 species of mammals.

野生动物中含国家一级保护动物黑颈鹤、东方白鹳、白冠长尾雉、云豹、穿山甲、大灵猫、小灵猫、丛林猫等，二级保护动物猕猴、游隼、豹猫、毛冠鹿、大鲵、白琵鹭、鸳鸯、苍鹰、黑鸢、白尾鹞、鹊鹞、凤头蜂鹰、雀鹰、松雀鹰、普通鵟、红角鸮、雕鸮、

毕节市威宁草海湿地公园的黑颈鹤
Black-necked Crane in Weining Caohai Lake, Bijie City

大方县雨冲古银杏树群
Ancient ginkgo tree cluster in Yuchong, Dafang County

灰林鸮、短耳鸮、红隼、灰鹤、白腹锦鸡、红腹锦鸡、斑羚、水獭、白鹇等，“三有”保护动物岩羊、豹猫、苍鹭等。

The wild animals in Bijie include the black-necked cranes, oriental white storks, white-crowned pheasants, clouded leopards, pangolins, civets, small civets, jungle cats, etc, which are national first-class protected species. And there are some second-class protected species, namely, rhesus monkeys, peregrine falcons, leopard cats, crested deer, giant salamanders, white spoonbill, mandarin duck, goshawk, black kite, white-tailed harrier, magpie harrier, crested humming hawk, sparrow hawk, pine sparrow hawk, buteo japonicus common buzzel, red screech owl, eagle owl, gray forest owl, short-eared owl, kestrel, gray crane, golden pheasant, golden pheasant, impala, otter, white pheasant, etc. There are also some "three haves" species (the protected species have significant ecological, scientific, or social value) like blue sheep, leopard cat, heron, etc.

植物资源：已查明的森林植物 862 种。其中苔藓植物 100 种，蕨类植物 130 种，木本植物 93 科 632 种（变种），内含一级保护植物光叶珙桐、云贵水韭、红豆杉、银杏等，二级保护植物篦子三尖杉、香果树、福建柏、鹅掌楸、水青树、翠柏、油杉、厚朴、闽楠、黄杉、红椿等。

So far, 862 species of forest plants have been identified in Bijie. Among them, there are 100 species of bryophytes, 130 species of ferns, and 632 species (variants) of 93 families of woody plants, including first-class protected plants, namely, Davidia glabrata, Yunnan-Guizhou water leek, yew, ginkgo, and others. Moreover, there are second-class protected plants, say, cephalotaxus fortunei, fragrant fruit tree, Fujian cypress, Liriodendron tulip tree, tetracentron sinensis, bluish green cypress, Yale fir, Magnolia officinalis, phoebe bournei, cedar, toona ciliata, among others.

水文资源 Hydrological Resources

毕节市河流均属山区雨源型河流，水资源量主要由降水补给，分属长江和珠江两大流域，境内长江流域面积共 25,614 平方千米、占 95.4%，有乌江（流经全市各区县）、赤水河（流经毕节

支格阿鲁湖 Zhigealu Lake

市七星关区、大方县、金沙县）、牛栏江（流经威宁彝族回族苗族自治县）和横江（流经威宁彝族回族苗族自治县和赫章县）四大水系。其中乌江有南、北两源，南源三岔河全长 346 千米，全流域面积 7,383 平方千米；北源六冲河干流全长 273 千米，全流域面积 10,874 平方千米。赤水河干流全长 506 千米，全流域面积 18,804 平方千米。牛栏江干流全长 484 千米，全流域面积 13,809 平方千米。横江干流全长 393 千米，全流域面积 14,914 平方千米。珠江流域面积 1,239 平方千米、占 4.6%，主要河流为可渡河（流经威宁彝族回族苗族自治县金钟镇）。全市集水面积 50 平方千米及以上河流 169 条，100 平方千米及以上河流 95 条，300 平方千米及以上河流 37 条，淡水湖泊 1 个（威宁草海）。

The rivers in Bijie City are all rain-fed rivers in mountainous areas, and their water resources are mainly supplied by precipitation, which belong to two major basins, the Yangtze River and the Pearl River. The total area of the Yangtze River basin is 25,614 square kilometers, accounting for 95.4% of the city's territory. There are four major water systems in the city: Wujiang River (flowing through the whole region), Chishuihe River (flowing through Qixingguan District, Dafang County, and Jinsha County), Niulanjiang River (flowing through Weining Yi, Hui and Miao Autonomous County) and Hengjiang River (flowing through Weining Yi, Hui and Miao Autonomous County and Hezhang County) . Among them, Wujiang River has two sources in the south and north. The Sancha River in the south has a total length of 346 kilometers, with a total drainage area of 7,383 square kilometers; the main stream of the Liuchonghe River in the north has a total length of 273 kilometers, with a total drainage area of 10,874 square kilometers. The main stream of the Chishuihe River is 506 kilometers long, with a basin area of 18,804 square kilometers. The main stream of the Niulanjiang River is 484 kilometers

美丽的乌江 Beautiful Wujiang River

long, with a basin area of 13,809 square kilometers. The main stream of the Hengjiang River is 393 kilometers long, with a basin area of 14,914 square kilometers. The Pearl River basin covers an area of 1,239 square kilometers, accounting for 4.6%. The main river is the Keduhe River (flowing through Jinzhong Town, Weining Yi, Hui, and Miao Autonomous County). The city has 169 rivers with a catchment area of 50 square kilometers and above, 95 rivers of 100 square kilometers and above, 37 rivers of 300 square kilometers and above. There is one freshwater lake, Weining Caohai.

风光资源 Wind and Solar Resources

西部大开发战略实施以来，毕节依托煤电产业的支柱作用，

充分发挥风力和太阳能资源优势，大力推动绿色清洁能源发展，正在走上一条水、火、风、光“四电”并举、一体推进的发展之路。

Since the implementation of the western development strategy, Bijie has relied on the pillar role of the coal-fired power, fully exploited the advantages of wind and solar energy resources, and vigorously promoted the development of green and clean energy. The city has made significant strides in promoting the growth of green and clean energy, and is currently utilizing an integrated approach to develop water, fire, wind, and light energy.

截至 2022 年底，全市已建成新能源项目 89 个、装机 514 万千瓦；在建新能源项目 16 个、装机 183.28 万千瓦；拟建新能源项目 90 个、装机 567.94 万千瓦。

光伏发电基地 Photovoltaic power generation base

By the end of 2022, the city has completed 89 new energy projects with an installed capacity of 5.14 million kilowatts; 16 new energy projects are under construction with an installed capacity of 1.8328 million kilowatts; 90 new energy projects are planned to be built with an installed capacity of 5.6794 million kilowatts.

新能源发电产业从无到有，装机规模从 2016 年的 140 万千瓦增加到 2022 年的 514 万千瓦，年均增加 53.4 万千瓦，装机规模占全市电力装机比重由 2016 年的 11.7% 增加到 2022 年的 32.4%，提升了 20.7%。新能源装机占全省的 25.5%，位列全省第一。

The new energy power generation industry has grown from scratch, and the installed capacity has increased from 1.4 million kilowatts in 2016 to 5.14 million kilowatts in 2022, with an average annual increase of 534,000 kilowatts. The proportion of installed capacity in the city's installed capacity has increased from 11.7% in

2016 increased to 32.4% in 2022 with an increase of 20.7%. New energy installed capacity accounts for 25.5% of the province's total installed capacity, ranking first in the province.

新能源发电量从 2016 年的 22.13 亿千瓦时增加到 2022 年的 71.88 亿千瓦时，年均增加 9.9 亿千瓦时，发电量占全市发电量的占比由 2016 年的 5.7% 增加到 2022 年的 14.3%，增加了 8.6%。

New energy power generation capacity increased from 2.213 billion kwh in 2016 to 7.188 billion kwh in 2022 with an average annual increase of 0.99 billion kwh, and the proportion of new energy power generation to the total power generation in the city rose from 5.7% to 14.3% in 2022, an increase of 8.6%.

毕节概览

2022

03

经济概况

Economy Overview

综合实力 Comprehensive Strength

根据市（州）生产总值统一核算结果，2022 年全市生产总值为 2,206.52 亿元。其中，第一产业增加值 551.35 亿元，第二产业增加值 560.13 亿元，第三产业增加值 1,095.04 亿元。

According to the unified accounting of the city's (or prefecture's) gross domestic product, the city's GDP reached to 220.652 billion yuan in 2022. The added value of the primary industry was 55.135 billion yuan while that of the secondary industry was 56.013 billion yuan, and the added value of the tertiary industry was 109.504 billion yuan.

工业指标 Industrial Indicators

2022 年，全市工业增加值 444.29 亿元。规模以上工业中，烟草制品业增加值比上年同期增长 5.8%，电力、热力生产和供应业增加值增长 1.5%，石油、煤炭及其他燃料加工业增加值增长

黔西煤化工厂区 Qianxi Coal Chemical Plant Area

毕节明钧玻璃生产线 Bijie Mingjun Glass Production Line

2.6%，纺织服装、服饰业增加值增长 25.8%，食品制造业增加值增长 10.3%，医药制造业增加值增长 7.8%，通用设备制造业增加值增长 78%，专用设备制造业增加值增长 255.6%。

In 2022, the added value of the industries in whole Bijie City reached 44.429 billion yuan. Among the industrial sectors above designated size, the added value of the tobacco industry increased by 5.8% compared to the same period of the preceding year. The electricity and heat production, and supply industry experienced a growth of 1.5% in the added value, while the petroleum, coal, and other fuel processing industry witnessed a 2.6% increase. The added value of the textile, apparel, and fashion industry saw a significant growth of 25.8% . The food manufacturing industry recorded a growth of 10.3%, and the pharmaceutical manufacturing industry experienced a rise of 7.8%. The general equipment manufacturing industry exhibited a substantial growth rate of 78%, and the specialized equipment manufacturing industry surged by an impressive 255.6%.

分产品看，原煤产量比上年同期增长 7.3%，乙二醇产量增长 17.9%，矿山专用设备产量增长 61.5%，白酒产量增长 6.2%，糖果产量增长 56.6%，服装产量增长 18.3%，皮革鞋靴产量增长 54.1%。

In terms of specific products, the production of coal and ethylene glycol increased respectively by 7.3% and 17.9% compared to the same period of the preceding year, while the output of mining specialized equipment saw a significant increase of 61.5%. Baijiu (Chinese liquor) experienced a growth rate of 6.2%. The production of candy, clothing, and leather footwear respectively grew by 56.6%, 18.3%, and 54.1%.

威宁雪榕食用菌大棚基地
Weining Xuerong Edible Mushroom Greenhouse Base

农业指标 Agricultural Indicators

2022年，全市农林牧渔业总产值921.25亿元。其中，种植业产值654.88亿元，林业产值34.02亿元，畜牧业产值192.49亿元，渔业产值3.23亿元。

In 2022, the city's total output value of agriculture, forestry, animal husbandry and fishery has mounted to 92.125 billion yuan. Among them, the output value of planting is 65.488 billion yuan, the output value of forestry is 3.402 billion yuan, the output value of animal

husbandry is 19.249 billion yuan, and the output value of fishery is 323 million yuan.

服务业指标 Tertiary Industrial Indicators

2022 年，全市服务业增加值 1,095.04 亿元，比上年同期增长 1.7%。道路运输业增加值增长 1.7%，全年平安运送旅客 1,559.59 万人次，公交出行量 1.1 亿人次。软件和信息技术服务业营业收入增长 35.6%。金融业增加值增长 4.4%，年末金融机构人民币各项存款余额 2,283.96 亿元，增长 10.7%，金融机构人民币各项贷款余额 2,814.11 亿元，增长 11.9%。邮政业增加值增长 1.5%，邮政行业业务总量 8.35 亿元，增长 6.9%，邮政行业业务收入 9.5 亿元，增长 9.1%。快递业务量 2,905.14 万件，增长 24.7%，快递业务收入 5.28 亿元，增长 7.7%。

In 2022, the added value of Bijie's service industry was 109.504 billion yuan, representing a growth rate of 1.7% compared to the same period of 2021. The added value of the industry of road transportation also increased by1.7%, providing a total of 15.5959 million safe trips. The public transportation service provided 110 million trips. The industry of softwarc and information technology services witnessed a substantial growth of 35.6% in business revenue. The growth rate of the financial industry was 4.4%. The total balance of RMB deposits in financial institutions at the end of the year amounted to 228.396 billion yuan, showing a 10.7% increase. The balance of RMB loans reached 281.411 billion yuan, reflecting an 11.9% growth rate. The added value of the postal industry increased by 1.5%. The total volume of the postal services reached 835 million, indicating a growth rate of 6.9%. The business revenue of the postal industry amounted to 950 million yuan, with a growth rate of 9.1%. The express delivery industry recorded a significant increase in business volume, reaching 29.0514 million yuan, demonstrating a growth rate of 24.7%. The business revenue of the express delivery industry amounted to 528 million yuan, increasing by 7.7%.

毕节概览
2022

04

基础设施

Infrastructure

铁路建设 Railway Construction

一列动车组列车从毕节市驶过
A high-speed train passing through Bijie City

铁路建成运营里程538千米（高铁125千米）。2019年，成贵高铁建成通车，毕节实现高铁“零”的突破，进入“高铁时代”。

The railway in operation is 538 kilometers (high-speed rail 125 kilometers). In 2019, the Chengdu-Guiyang high-speed rail was completed and opened to traffic, marking a breakthrough for Bijie as it entered the "high-speed railway era" with access to high-speed rail for the first time.

公路建设 Road Construction

截至2022年末，全市公路通车里程达34,482.6千米，高速公路“县县通”、里程达1,086千米，普通国道二级公路比例达99.07%，普通省道三级及以上公路比例达56.54%，建制村100%通沥青（水泥）路和通客运，30户以上的自然村寨100%通硬化路。大方县、黔西市、百里杜鹃管理区被评为“四好农村路”省级示范县。

By the end of 2022, road mileage has reached 34,482.6 kilometers. All counties in Bijie have been connected with the expressway of

四通八达的公路网 A road network that extends in all directions

1,086 mileage, 99.07 % of the national roads have reached the second-class level. 56.54% of the provincial roads have reached the third-class level. All administrative villages have been connected by asphalt or cement roads. 100% of villages with more than 30 households have been connected by the hardened roads. Dafang County, Qianxi City, and Baili Azalea National Forest Park Management Zone were appraised as provincial example of " Four Excellences in constructing countryside roads".

机场建设 Airport Construction

2013 年，毕节飞雄机场建成通航，毕节实现航空“零”的突破，进入“航空时代”。为满足旅客吞吐量需求，毕节飞雄机场改扩建工程已于 2020 年正式开工建设，预计 2024 年完工。

In 2013, the Bijie Feixiong Airport was completed and opened for air traffic, representing a significant milestone in aviation for Bijie as it entered the "aviation era". In order to accommodate the growing demand

毕节飞雄机场改扩建工程项目建设效果图
Architectural rendering of a reconstruction and expansion project of Bijie Feixiong Airport

for passenger throughput, the expansion project for Bijie Feixiong Airport began in 2020, with an expected completion date of 2024.

贵州威宁民用机场于 2019 年 3 月 23 日开工建设，预计 2023 年 10 月底完成全部主体工程建设。

Construction of the Guizhou Weining Civil Airport began on March 23, 2019 and is projected to complete all primary construction projects by the end of October 2023.

水利建设 Water Conservancy Construction

截至 2022 年底，全市已建成各类水利水务设施共 7,844 处。全市已建水库 206 座，总库容 17.28 亿立方米，设计供水量 10.49 亿立方米。其中，大型水库 1 座（夹岩水利枢纽及黔西北供水工程），总库容 13.23 亿立方米，设计供水量 6.07 亿立方米；中型水库 13 座，总库容 2.17 亿立方米，设计供水量 2.57 亿立方米；小型水库 192 座，总库容 1.88 亿立方米，设计供水量 1.85 亿立方米。

By the end of 2022, a total of 7,844 water conservancy and water facilities have been built. And the city has built 206 reservoirs with a total storage capacity of 1.728 billion cubic meters and a designed water supply of 1.049 billion cubic meters. Among them, there is one large-scale reservoir (Jiayan Water Conservancy Project and Northwest Guizhou Water Supply Project), with a total storage capacity of 1.323 billion cubic meters and a designed water supply of 607 million cubic meters; 13 medium-sized reservoirs with a total storage capacity of 217 million cubic meters and a designed water supply of 257 million cubic meters cubic meters; 192 small reservoirs with a total storage capacity of 188 million cubic meters and a designed water supply of 185 million cubic meters.

在建中小型水库 33 座（中型 7 座、小型 26 座），总投资 86.35 亿元，总库容 2.10 亿立方米。

夹岩水利枢纽工程 Jiayan Water Conservancy Project

Currently, 33 small and medium-sized reservoirs are under construction (7 medium-sized and 26 small-sized), with a total investment of 8.635 billion yuan and a total storage capacity of 210 million cubic meters.

电力建设 Power Construction

2012 年以来，南方电网毕节供电局累计投资 123.75 亿元，用于毕节市电网建设，总投资位列全省第一。

Since 2012, the Bijie Power Supply Bureau of China Southern Power Grid has invested a total of 12.375 billion yuan in constructing Bijie power grid, ranking first in the province in terms of total investment.

10 年来，毕节供电局重点建成投运了威宁 500 千伏乌撒输变电工程、500 千伏奢香输变电工程、500 千伏奢香至鸭溪输变电工程等，实现 220 千伏变电站县域全覆盖，为服务毕节市能源产业高质量发展提供了坚实的电力支撑。

500 千伏乌撒变电站 500 kV Wusa Substation

500 千伏奢香变电站 500 kV Shexiang Substation

In the past 10 years, the Bijie Power Supply Bureau has focused on the completion and operation of the Weining 500 kV Wusa Power Transmission and Transformation Project, the 500 kV Shexiang Power Transmission and Transformation Project, and the 500 kV Shexiang to Yaxi Power Transmission and Transformation Project. At present, 220 thousand voltage substations cover all counties, providing a solid power support for serving the high-quality development of Bijie City.

截至 2022 年底，毕节电网 35 千伏及以上变电站共有 192 座（其中 500 千伏变电站 2 座、220 千伏变电站 10 座、110 千伏及以下变电站 180 座），主变容量 1,321.1 万千伏安。10 千伏及以上线路 1,488 条，总长 4.1205 万千米，公用配变 35,879 台，容量 617.2507 万千伏安。毕节电网形成了以 500 千伏奢香输变电工程、乌撒输变电工程为支撑，10 座 220 千伏变电站为骨干的坚强网架，实现与贵阳、遵义、水城电网联络，加快推进安全、可靠、绿色、高效、智能的现代化电网建设，为毕节市建设贯彻新发展理念示范区提供了坚强的“电力引擎”。

By the end of 2022, there will be 192 substations of 35 kV and above (including 2 substations of 500 kV, 10 substations of 220 kV, and 180 substations of 110 kV and below), the main transformer capacity of 1,321.1kVA. 10 kV and above, 1,488 kV lines with the total length of 41,205 kilometers, 35,879 units of public distribution transformers with capacity of 6.172507million kVA. Thus, it has formed a strong grid supported by the 500 kV Shexiang Power Transmission and Transformation Project and Wusa Power Transmission and Transformation Project, and 10 220 kV substations, which serves as the backbone. The grid is interconnected with those of Guiyang, Zunyi, and Shuicheng to expedite the development of a modern, safe, reliable, green, efficient, and intelligent power grid, serving as a potent "power engine" for the demonstration area of Bijie City and its implementation of the new development philosophy.

城市建设 Urban Construction

毕节市坚持旧城改造和新区开发并重，大力实施以城市“四改”为主要抓手的城市更新行动，推动黔西市南部新区、金沙县新城区、织金县绮陌新区、百里杜鹃管理区花海文化城等10个县城新区建设，不断补齐城市基础设施及公共服务设施短板。

Bijie City insists on equal emphasis on the renovation of old cities and the development of new districts, vigorously implements the urban renewal action with the "four improvements" in the city as the focus, and promotes the construction of 10 new county towns, including the southern new districts of Qianxi City, the new districts of Jinsha County, the Qimo District of Zhijin County and Huahai Cultural City

俯瞰金沙县 Overlooking Jinsha County

毕节城区新貌 New Appearance of Bijie Urban Area

in Baili Dujuan Management District.The aim of these sustained efforts is to address shortcomings in urban infrastructure and public services.

近年来，全市累计改造棚户区 26.13 万户、老旧小区 3.71 万户。南山体育公园、天河广场等重点项目建成使用，建成城市公园广场 53 个，人均公园绿地面积达 13.07 平方米。建成 4 个垃圾焚烧发电项目，新增垃圾处理能力 3,200 吨 / 日，全市垃圾处理能力达 4,600 吨 / 日。全市环境空气质量平均优良天数比例达 98.4%。

Recently, the city has transformed a total of 261,300 households in shantytowns and 37,100 households in old communities. Key projects, namely, Nanshan Sports Park and Tianhe Plaza have been completed and put into use, and 53 urban park squares were built, with a per capita park green area of 13.07 square meters. 4 waste incineration power generation projects have been built, and the newly added waste treatment capacity is 3,200 tons/day, bringing the city's waste treatment

capacity to 4,600 tons/day. The average number of days with good ambient air quality in the city has reached 98.4%.

到 2022 年底，全市城市建成区面积达 231.24 平方千米，成功创建“全国双拥模范城市”“国家卫生城市”“省级园林城市”，城市品质得到有效提升，城市综合承载能力和吸引力稳步增强，为实现“强市升位、跨越发展”打下了坚实基础。

By the end of 2022, the city's urban built-up area has expanded to 231.24 square kilometers, and has been successfully recognized as a "National Double Support Model City", "National Sanitation City" and "Provincial Garden City", and the city's quality has been effectively improved. The carrying capacity and attractiveness have been steadily enhanced, laying a solid foundation for achieving strong city promotion and leaping development.

毕节概览

2022

05

民生保障

Livelihood Security

科技 Science and Technology

2022年，毕节市抢抓国发［2022］2号和国函［2022］65号文件、“科技入黔”、东西部协作的政策机遇，获得贵州省科技厅立项支持24项。13家企业获得贵州省科技厅规上工业企业研发活动扶持计划支持。获得广州市科技局科技项目2项。

In 2022, Bijie City took advantage of policy opportunities presented by the State Council's " No.2 document of Guo Fa[2022] and " No. 65 document of Guo Han [2022]", as well as the "Science and Technology Enter Guizhou" initiative and inter-regional cooperation efforts between the east and west of China. These actions resulted in obtaining support for 24 projects from the Guizhou Provincial Department of Science and Technology. Additionally, 13 companies were supported by the department's R&D program for large-scale industrial enterprises,winning two projects from Guangzhou Science and Technology Bureau.

工人在贵州联尚科技有限公司生产车间内操作设备进行生产
Workers operating equipments in the production workshop of Guizhou Lianshang Technology Co. Ltd

全市“三上”企业中有研究与试验发展活动的企业93家，有高新技术企业44家，共登记技术合同919项，合同成交额44.8亿元。建设3家众创空间、1家科技企业孵化器和1个重点实验室等市级创新创业平台。全市首个新型研发机构——贵州致福光谷光电子信息产业研究院注册成立。率先在全省开展“科技特派员之家”建设，为各级科技特派员提供了工作、生活的后勤保障。

There are 93 "three upper" enterprises in the city engaged in research and experimental development activities, with 44 high-tech firms. A total of 919 technical contracts have been registered, with a transaction volume of 4.48 billion yuan. The city has established municipal innovation and entrepreneurship platforms, including three public innovation spaces, one science and technology business incubator, and one key laboratory. The Guizhou ZhiFu Guanggu Photoelectron Information Industry Research Institute, the city's first new R&D institution, has been successfully registered and established. Bijie City has taken the lead in developing the "Home of Science and

市民在毕节AI数字会客厅体验毕节景色
Citizen experiencing Bijie scenery in the Bijie AI Digital Reception Hall

Technology Commissioners" in the province, providing logistical support for all levels of Science and Technology Commissioners.

教育 Education

2022 年，全市有各级各类学校 4,581 所。其中幼儿园 2,449 所，小学 1,633 所，初级中学 297 所，九年一贯制学校 79 所，完全中学 38 所，高级中学 40 所，十二年一贯制学校 9 所，中等职业学校 15 所，特殊教育学校 9 所，专科学校 5 所，高等院校 6 所，

贵州工程应用技术学院 Guizhou University of Engineering Science

成人高等院校 1 所。有专任教师 108,160 人，在校生 1,836,473 人。全市坚决贯彻党的教育方针，落实立德树人的根本任务，坚持示范引领促发展，赫章县第一幼儿园创建为三类省级示范园，织金县城南幼儿园升级为二类省级示范园，黔西市锦绣恒大中心幼儿园通过省级示范园初评；市实验高中、赫章一中通过省级示范性高中初评。

By 2022, there were a total of 4,581 schools at all levels in the city, consisting of 2,449 kindergartens, 1,633 primary schools, 297 junior high schools, 79 nine-year comprehensive schools, 38 complete middle schools, 40 senior high schools, 9 twelve-year comprehensive

毕节职教城鸟瞰图
Aerial View of Bijie Vocational Education City

schools, 15 secondary vocational schools, 9 special education schools, 5 specialized schools, 6 institutions of higher learning, and 1 adult institution of higher learning. The enrollment included 108,160 full-time teachers and 1,836,473 students. The city is committed to implementing the educational policies of the Party, fulfilling the fundamental mission of fostering moral citizens, and promoting development through demonstration and guidance. Hezhang County's first kindergarten has been recognized as a provincial-level demonstration kindergarten, while the South City Kindergarten in Zhijin County was upgraded to a second-class provincial demonstration kindergarten. Jinxiu Hengda Central Kindergarten in Qianxi City passed the preliminary evaluation as a provincial-level demonstration kindergarten. The Municipal Experimental High School and Hezhang No.1 High School have also secured preliminary evaluations as provincial-level demonstration high schools.

强化能力素质提升，在各种竞赛中彰显教育本色。在贵州省第五届学生运动会田径项目中，毕节市选派的 20 名运动员，获得了6金、7银、5铜的好成绩，并夺得全省中学组团体总分第二名。在全国职业院校技能大赛中，毕节市参赛选手获国家级技能大赛奖4项、省级技能大赛奖81项。

Bijie City has attached great importance of improving students' abilities and qualities, and highlighting the educational essence through various competitions. At the fifth Guizhou Provincial Student Athletic Meet, 20 athletes from Bijie City won a total of 6 gold, 7 silver, and 5 bronze medals, in the track and field events, placing second overall in the secondary school group. In the national vocational college skills competition, participants from Bijie City won 4 awards at the national level and 81 awards at the provincial level.

文化 Culture

“十三五”以来，毕节市坚持“资源下沉，重点下移”，强力推进基层公共文化场所设施、服务供给、人才队伍等建设，成功获得国家级示范区的命名授牌。

Since the 13th Five-Year Plan, Bijie City has been committed to the principle of "resource allocation and focus shifting", making great efforts to improve the facilities, service supply, and talent pool of public cultural institutions at the grassroots level. As a result of these efforts, the city was successfully awarded the title of National Demonstration Zone.

基层文化设施日臻完善。新建县级文化馆2个、图书馆2个，提升改造县级文化馆7个、图书馆7个。新建乡（镇、街道）综合文化站34个，新建、改扩建、整合设置村（社区）综合文化服务中心1,383个，新建文体广场1,106个。142个集中安置区文化服务中心设置率达100%。因地制宜设置讲习所、图书室、“四

村民在贵州省毕节市大方县八堡乡复兴村农家书屋里阅读图书
Villagers reading books in the rural library of Fuxing Village, Babao Township, Dafang County, Bijie City, Guizhou Province

点半学校”、乡愁馆、文化广场，配备文化广电体育设备。市、县、乡、村四级数字文化设施和无线网络全覆盖，建成“毕节文化云”数字服务平台和贵州省首个数字虚拟博物馆。

The cultural infrastructure at the grassroots level has been greatly enhanced. Two new county-level cultural centers and two libraries have been constructed, while seven county-level cultural centers and seven libraries have been renovated and upgraded. In addition, 34 comprehensive cultural stations have been established in townships (towns and streets), together with 1,383 newly-built or improved village and community cultural service centers, and 1,106 new sports and cultural squares. The cultural service centers in 142 centralized resettlement areas have achieved an impressive 100% coverage rate, which includes study rooms, libraries, "4:30 schools", nostalgia halls, cultural squares, and cultural, radio, and sports facilities that are customized according to local conditions. The digital cultural facilities and wireless networks have achieved full coverage at the city, county, township, and village levels. Furthermore, the "Bijie Cultural Cloud" digital service platform and Guizhou province's first digital virtual museum have also been established.

公共文化服务供给不断丰富。全市图书馆总藏书量 591.62 万册，年人均到馆次数从 0.38 次提高到 0.66 次。连续 8 年举办乌蒙文化艺术周、连续 6 年举办送文化下乡“百场演艺工程”、连续 3 年举办本土音乐广场舞大赛等市级品牌服务项目。

The supply of public cultural services is constantly enriched. The total collection of books in the city's libraries has reached 5.9162 million volumes, and the average number of visits per person has increased from 0.38 to 0.66. For eight years in a row, the Wumeng

黔西市新仁苗族乡折溪小学，当地苗绣蜡染传承人彭艺指导学生刺绣
Peng Yi, the inheritor of Miao embroidery and wax dyeing, tutoring students in embroidery in Zhexi Primary School, Xinren Miao Township, Qianxi City

Cultural and Art Festival has been held, as well as the "Hundred Performances Project" that brings cultural performances to rural areas for six consecutive years. Additionally, the city-level brand service project, the local music and square dance competition, has been held for three consecutive years.

文艺精品不断涌现。“十三五”以来，通过乌蒙文化艺术大赛等平台共推出优秀作品1,000余件。2022年，音乐作品《守望·撒麻》荣获全国群众文艺领域的政府最高奖项——群星奖。这是自群星奖创办31年来，毕节市音乐作品首次获奖，也是贵州省近十年来首次获奖。

An unceasing flow of excellent literary and artistic works has emerged. Since the advent of the 13th Five-Year Plan, over 1,000 outstanding works have been collaboratively launched through platforms such as the Wumeng Cultural and Art Competition. In 2022,

《守望 · 撒麻》剧照 A still from "*Watch Sama*"

the music work "*Watch Sama*" was awarded the highest government accolade in the field of mass literature and art – Stars Award. This marks the first-ever occasion that a musical work from Bijie City has received the honor in its 31-year history, and the first time in almost ten years that a work from Guizhou Province has been awarded.

卫生 Health

截至 2022 年末，全市共有医疗卫生机构 5,610 个。其中医院 315 个，基层医疗卫生机构 5,258 个，其中社区服务中心（站）53 个、乡（镇、街道）卫生院 251 个、村卫生室 4,492 个、门诊诊所等 462 个；专业公共卫生机构 33 个，其中疾控中心 10 个、妇幼保健院 10 个、急救中心 1 个、采供血机构 4 个、卫生健康综合行政执法机构 8 个。

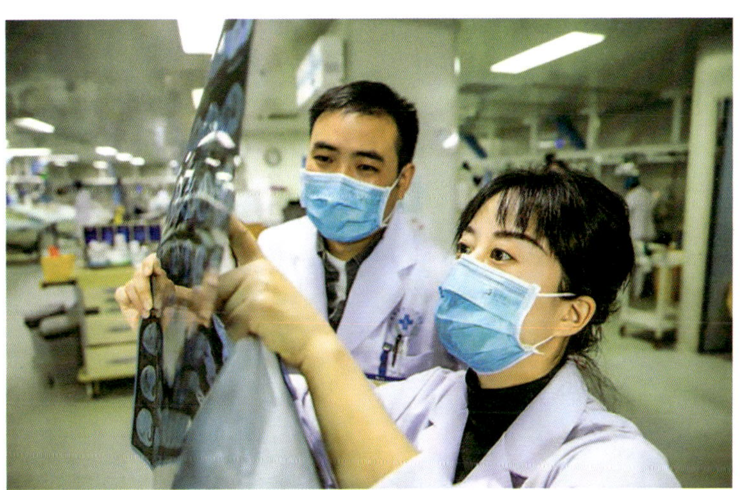

贵州省毕节市第一人民医院重症医学科医生在讨论患者病情
Doctors discussing symptoms in the Intensive Care Department of Bijie First People's Hospital, Guizhou Province

先天性心脏病筛查
Congenital heart defect screening

By the end of 2022, there are 5,610 medical and health institutions in the city, including 315 hospitals, and 5,258 primary health care institutions, among which we have 53 community service centers (stations), 251 township (subdistrict) clinics, and 4,492 village clinics, and 462 outpatient clinics. There are 33 professional public health agencies, including 10 CDCs, 10 MCH hospitals, 1 emergency center, 4 blood collection and supply institutions, and 8 comprehensive administrative law enforcement agencies for health.

全市医疗机构共有床位数 51,717 张，执业（助理）医师 16,129 人，注册护士 22,359 人，注册全科医师 1,376 名。以 2022 年末常住人口 681.59 万人计算，全市每千人（常住人口）床位数 7.59 张、执业（助理）医师 2.37 人、注册护士 3.28 人。

In total, the medical institutions in the city have 51,717 beds, 16,129 licensed (assistant) physicians, 22,359 registered nurses, and 1,376 registered general practitioners. Based on the permanent resident population of 6.8159 million in the end of 2022, there are 7.59 beds, 2.37 licensed (assistant) physicians, and 3.28 registered nurses per thousand people in the city.

体育 Sports

2022 年，毕节市紧扣新时代体育事业发展目标，推动群众体育、竞技体育、体育产业等齐头并进。市县两级举办、承办了赛事活动 150 余场（次），覆盖群众 100 余万人（次）。毕节代表团在贵州省第十一届运动会上取得奖牌数和金牌数全省第三的好成绩。在“菲普莱杯”全国 U18 田径锦标赛上，毕节运动员吕大春夺冠，拿下了毕节运动员近十年来的第一枚全国田径锦标赛场地赛金牌。

“元宝女足”合影 Yuanbao Women's Football Team

2022 年 6 月 4 日，贵州省第七届速度轮滑公开赛在百里杜鹃举行
The 7th Guizhou Speed Roller Skating Open in Baili Azalea National Forest Park on June 4, 2022

In 2022, Bijie City pursued the development goals of the new era of sports industry and promoted the coordinated progress of mass sports, competitive sports, and the sports industry. A total of more than 150 sports events were held and hosted at the city and county levels, covering more than one million participants. The Bijie delegation ranked the third place of the total number of medals and gold medals at the 11th Guizhou Provincial Games. Additionally, at the "Feipulei Cup" National U18 Athletics Championship, Lü Dachun from Bijie claimed victory with a remarkable. This was the first gold medal earned by the athlete from Bijie in the national events in the past decade.

积极打造体育运动基地，推动体育事业再上新台阶。遵义赤水·乌蒙体育旅游线路入选“2022 年国庆假期体育旅游精品线路”，毕节“磅礴乌蒙”户外休闲运动体育旅游线路入选“2023 年春节假期体育旅游精品线路”，百里杜鹃全国山地自行车邀请赛入选 2022 年中国体育旅游精品项目。2022 年 12 月 12 日，贵州省体育局授予威宁“贵州省高原体育训练基地”称号。

Efforts have been made to construct sports training facilities and drive the development of the sports industry to a new height. Zunyi Chishui Wumeng Sports Tourism Route was selected as the "2022 National Day Holiday Sports Tourism Boutique Route", Bijie's outdoor leisure sports tourism route "Breathtaking Wumeng" was chosen as a "2023 Spring Festival Sports Tourism Boutique Route", National Mountain Bike Invitational in Baili Azalea National Forest Park was selected as a 2022 China Sports Tourism Boutique Project. On December 12, 2022, the Guizhou Provincial Sports Bureau awarded Weining the honor of being the "Guizhou Plateau Sports Training Base".

威宁草海半程马拉松赛欢乐跑第一名到达终点

The champion crossed the finish line at the Winning Caohai Half Marathon

社会保障 Social Security

深入实施全民参保计划，全民参保覆盖面持续扩大。截至 2022 年底，全市城镇职工基本养老保险参保 64.42 万人，失业保险参保 33.5 万人，工伤保险参保 70.45 万人，城乡居民基本养老保险参保 387.05 万人。

Efforts are being made to vigorously implement the universal social insurance plan and expand its coverage. By the end of 2022, a total of 644,200 urban employees were covered by basic endowment insurance, 335,000 people were covered by unemployment insurance, 704,500 people were covered by work-related injury insurance, and basic endowment insurance for both urban and rural residents covered as many as 3,870,500 people in Bijie City.

市民体验智慧医疗 Citizen experiencing smart healthcare

村民在贵州省毕节市七星关区响水乡青山村辣椒加工厂劳作
Villagers working in the chili pepper processing factory, Qingshan Village, Xiangshui Township, Qixingguan District, Bijie City, Guizhou Province

全面落实助企纾困优惠政策。2022年，累计为1.9万家企业（单位）“降缓返补”各类社保资金5.53亿元，惠及职工105.71万人。

Bijie City fully implemented preferential policies to assist enterprises and ease their difficulties. In 2022, a total of 19,000 enterprises (units) have received a total of 553 million yuan in various social security funds through measures such as reduction, deferment, return, and subsidy, benefiting 1.0571 million employees.

加强数字技术的使用，不断优化为民服务水平，提升公共服务效能。加快推进社保卡居民服务“一卡通”建设，在383个银行网点开通社会保障卡办理业务。深入推进“全省通办”“跨省通办”“一窗通办‘2＋2’模式”改革，全力打造“贵人服务·毕须办”政务服务品牌和群众满意的人社服务。

Bijie City aims to enhance our use of digital technology, continuously optimize public services, and elevate the efficiency and quality of such services. It will expedite the development of the "one-card-for-all" social security card system, and provide social security card processing services at 383 bank outlets. Moreover, it is committed to advancing the reform of the "province-wide service", "inter-provincial service" and "2 + 2 window service" models, and strive to establish a government service brand, as well as people-oriented social security services which meet public satisfaction.

人民生活 People's Lives

2022 年，毕节市扎实推进促进居民增收三年行动，持续保障和改善民生，城乡居民收入稳步增长。全市城镇常住居民人均可支配收入 39,055 元，同比增长 4.8%，农村常住居民人均可支配收入 13,245 元，同比增长 6.5%。全市城镇常住居民人均消费支出 20,878 元，农村常住居民人均消费支出 12,293 元。

In 2022, Bijie City firmly executed the three-year action plan aimed at boosting residents' earnings, continuously ensuring and

广场舞 Square dancing

enhancing their living standards, while progressively increasing the income of both urban and rural inhabitants. The per capita disposable income of urban permanent residents in Bijie was 39,055 yuan, representing a year-on-year growth rate of 4.8%. Rural residents, on the other hand, had an average disposable income of 13,245 yuan, with a growth rate of 6.5%. Moreover, urban residents in the city had an average consumer expenditure of 20,878 yuan, while rural residents had an average consumer expenditure of 12,293 yuan.

毕节概览
2022

06

旅游文化

Tourism Culture

景区景点 Scenic Spots

百里杜鹃 Baili Azalea National Forest Park

百里杜鹃景区地处贵州省西北部、毕节市中部，距贵阳高铁北站106千米、毕节飞雄机场45千米、黔西高铁站32千米、大方高铁站31千米。杭瑞高速、黔大高速、成贵快铁穿境而过。景区占地面积697.174平方千米，人口15.08万人。

Baili Azalea National Forest Park is located in the northwest of Guizhou Province and the center of Bijie City, 106 kilometers away from Guiyang North Railway Station, 45 kilometers from Bijie Feixiong

百里杜鹃景区 Baili Azalea National Forest Park

Airport, 32 kilometers from Qianxi Railway Station and 31 kilometers from Dafang Railway Station. The Hangrui Expressway, Qianda Expressway, and Chenggui high-speed Railway pass through its border. The scenic area covers an area of 697.174 square kilometers and has a population of 150,800 people.

百里杜鹃拥有世界上面积最大、品种最多、景观最震撼的原始杜鹃林带，绵延 125.8 平方千米。百里杜鹃景区包括普底景区、金坡景区、戛木景区、花王景区、百合景区，其中核心游览景区为普底景区、金坡景区，原生杜鹃花延绵百里，是迄今为止已查明的世界上面积最大、种类最多、保存最完好的原始杜鹃林，堪称世界唯一。

百里杜鹃景区 Baili Azalea National Forest Park

Baili Azalea National Forest Park has the world's largest, most diverse, and most stunning pristine azalea forest belt, stretching 125.8 square kilometers. It consists of Pudi Scenic Area, Jinpo Scenic Area, Gamu Scenic Area, Huawang Scenic Area, and Baihe Scenic Area. The core tourist attractions are Pudi Scenic Area and Jinpo Scenic Area, with original azalea stretching for hundreds of miles. It is the widest, most various, and best-preserved primitive azalea forest in the world identified so far, and can be considered the only one in the world.

暮春时节，各种杜鹃花争相怒放，千姿百态，色彩缤纷，姹紫嫣红。绚烂花海形成一幅气势恢宏的画卷，在崇山峻岭间腾挪跌宕，绵延百里，形成了世界上罕见的自然景观，被誉为“地球彩带、杜鹃王国”。每年的 3—5 月是最佳观花期，不同花形、不同颜色的杜鹃花在阳光的沐浴下，竞相绽放在绿色枝头，红、粉、紫、金、黄、绿交相辉映。置身林间花径，能让人感受“花香醉游客，鸟语惊人梦”的山水之乐。

In late spring, various azaleas are in full bloom, with diverse forms and colorful hues. The gorgeous sea of flowers forms a magnificent picture, which stretches for hundreds of li among the mountains, forming a rare natural landscape in the world, known as "the earth ribbon" and " the azalea kingdom". March to May is the best season to enjoy azalea blossoms each year. Azaleas of different shapes and colors bloom on green branches in the sunlight, with red, pink, purple, gold, yellow, and green complementing each other. Walking along the flower path in the forest, tourists can experience the joy of "intoxicating fragrance of the flowers and mellifluous singing of the birds".

织金洞 Zhijin Cave

织金洞世界地质公园位于贵州省织金县，是贵州首家世界地质公园，是中国最美溶洞、国家级风景名胜区、国家地质公园、国家自然遗产、国家 AAAAA 级旅游景区。

织金洞灵芝山、桫椤树景观
Lingzhi Mountain and Suoluo Tree Landscape in Zhijin Cave

织金洞霸王盔景观 The King's Helmet Landscape in Zhijin Cave

Zhijin Cave Geopark is located in Zhijin County, Guizhou Province. It is the first world geopark in Guizhou Province and the most beautiful karst cave in China. It is also a national scenic spot, a national geopark, a national natural heritage, and a national 5A-level tourist attraction.

1980 年 4 月，织金洞景区被发现。1988 年，国务院将织金洞景区审定为第二批国家级风景名胜区。2013 年，织金洞景区被评为“最美地质公园”。2015 年 9 月 19 日，织金洞国家地质公园被联合国教科文组织正式批准列入世界地质公园网络名录。

In April 1980, Zhijin Cave was discovered. In 1988, the State Council approved Zhijin Cave Scenic Area as the Second Batch of National Level Scenic Spots. In 2013, Zhijin Cave Scenic Area was rated as the "Most Beautiful Geopark". On September 19, 2015, Zhijin Cave National Geopark was officially added to the list of UNESCO Global Geoparks.

织金洞世界地质公园具有独特的地质遗迹特征和极高的审美

织金洞寿星宫 · 万家灯火景观
Shouxing Palace and Wanjia Lantern Landscape in Zhijin Cave

价值，用三个字来概括就是“大、奇、全”。

The Zhijin Cave Geopark has unique geological heritage characteristics and extremely high aesthetic value, which can be summarized in three words as "large, unique, and comprehensive".

“大”是指织金洞的空间及景观规模宏伟，气魄大，洞体两壁高宽处为 175 米，相对高差 150 米，一般高宽均在 60 — 100 米，大小厅堂 47 个，其中上万平方米的厅堂有 5 个。

"Large" refers to the grand and magnificent spatial and landscape scale of the Zhijin Cave. The height and width of the cave are about 175 meters, with a relative height difference of 150 meters. Generally, the height and width are between 60-100 meters, and there are 47 halls of different sizes, including 5 halls of tens of thousands of square meters.

“奇”是指景物及空间造型奇特，像银雨树、霸王盔、倒挂琵琶、大壁画、姊妹玉树等景观栩栩如生。

"Unique" refers to the distinctive scenery and rock shape, such as the Silver Rain Tree, the King's Helmet, the Inverted Pipa, the Large Mural, and Stalactite Sisters, which are lifelike landscapes.

“全”是指洞内景物形态丰富，囊括了全世界溶洞的主要形态和类别，有石墙、石笋、月奶石、边石坝、卷曲石、石花、壁流石等，具有极高的科研价值。

"Comprehensive" describes the diverse range of cave formations found within Zhijin Cave, which encompasses major forms and categories of karst caves from around the world. These include stone walls, stalactites, moonmilk, rimstone dams, helictites, stone flowers, flowstones, and other formations. The cave formations have significant scientific research value.

乌江源百里画廊 Baili Gallery of Wujiang River Source

乌江源百里画廊位于黔西市南部，因修建东风水电站而形成。

乌江源百里画廊东风湖景区
Dongfeng Lake Scenic Area, Baili Gallery of Wujiang River Source

东风湖区总长 62 千米，宽度 60 — 1,000 米，湖水面积近 20 平方千米，江水两岸峰壁险峻，多瀑布山泉跌落湖中，是千里乌江上最美的崖壁画廊。处于该流域的化屋苗寨是“贵州苗族歌舞之乡”，芦笙拳舞和多声部合唱是其独特的演艺形式，以东风湖、化屋苗寨为典型代表。

Baili Gallery of Wujiang River Source is located in the south of Qianxi City and formed due to the construction of Dongfeng Hydropower Plant. The Dongfeng Lake District is 62 kilometers long and 60-1,000 meters wide, covering nearly 20 square kilometers. The peaks on both sides of the river are steep and dangerous, with many waterfalls and springs falling into the lake. This is the most beautiful cliff gallery on the thousand-mile Wujiang River. Huawu Miao Village, located in this watershed, is the "hometown of Guizhou Miao ethnic songs and dances". Lusheng Dance and multi voice choir are the unique performance forms of the Miao ethnic group in the Wujiang Rive basin, where Dongfeng Lake and Huawu Miao Village are typical representatives.

乌江源百里画廊 Baili Gallery of Wujiang River Source

韭菜坪 Jiucaiping Scenic Area

阿西里西 · 韭菜坪景区，又称大韭菜坪景区，位于贵州省赫章县西南部兴发苗族彝族回族乡、水塘堡彝族苗族乡、白果街道接合部，距毕威高速公路赫章站出口约 30 千米，海拔为 2,300 — 2,778 米，主峰海拔 2,778 米，是贵州第五高峰。景区面积 80 平方千米，2017 年 8 月获国家 AAAA 级旅游景区授牌。

Axilixi Jiucaiping Scenic Area, also known as Dajiucaiping Scenic Area, is located at the junction of Xingfa Miao, Yi and Hui Ethnic Township, Shuitangbao Yi and Miao Ethnic Township, and Baiguo Street in the southwest of Hezhang County, Guizhou Province. It is about 30 kilometers away from the exit of Hezhang Station of the Biwei Expressway, and is at an elevation of 2,300-2,778 meters. The main peak is at an elevation of 2,778 meters and is the fifth highest peak in Guizhou. With an area of 80 square kilometers, the scenic area was awarded the National 4A-level Tourist Attraction in August 2017.

夕阳下的韭菜坪 Jiucaiping under the setting sun

天上花海 Flower Sea

景区以十万余亩长满野生韭菜的高原平台为主体，是世界上面积最大的连片野生韭菜花带，是全国唯一的野生韭菜花保护区，有“中国野生韭菜——多星韭之乡”之称，具有极高的科研价值和美学价值，被誉为“地球的蓝宝石，东方的普罗旺斯”。韭菜坪景区也是“山地公园省·多彩贵州风”的典型代表、“洞天福地·花海毕节”的重要组成部分。

The scenic area is mainly composed of a plateau platform covered with over 100,000 acres of wild chives. It is the largest wild chive flower belt in the world and the only wild chive flower reserve in China. It is known as the "Hometown of Chinese Wild Chives - Multi Star Chives" and has great scientific and aesthetic value, known as the "Sapphire of the Earth" and "Provence of the East". Jiucaiping Scenic Area is also a typical representative of "Mountain Park Province · Colorful Guizhou Style" and an important component of "Dongtian Blessed Land · Bijie Flower Sea".

“不到韭菜坪，枉看贵州山。”景区春夏秋冬四时美景各异，变化神奇，特别是韭菜花海、云海日出、万顷峰丛、阴涧岩壁、高原冰雪等景色尤为壮观。伫立景区，向远处看，广阔蓝天下是一幅“万峰藏云下，人在云上行”的神奇画卷；向脚下看，群山

黎明时的韭菜坪风光 The scenery of Jiucaiping at dawn

沟壑尽收眼底，“会当凌绝顶，一览众山小”的韵味油然而生。

A saying goes that if you don't go to Jiucaiping, you will miss the charm of mountains in Guizhou. The scenic area has different beautiful scenery in spring, summer, autumn, and winter, especially the sea of chive flowers, the sea of clouds and sunrise, the thousands of hectares of peak clusters, the streams and cliffs, and the plateau ice and snow, which are particularly spectacular. Standing in the scenic area, you can enjoy a magical picture of "thousands of peaks hide under the clouds, and people ascend in the clouds" under the vast blue sky; overlooking the mountains and gullies, you can experience the charm depicted in the famous verse of "Try to ascend the mountain's crest, it dwarfs all peaks under our foot".

九洞天 Jiudongtian

九洞天国家级风景名胜区由总溪河碧水长廊景区、梯子岩层峦叠嶂景区、九洞天云洞天开景区组成，总面积 145 平方千米。景区距毕节市 75 千米，距大方县 54 千米，距纳雍县 60 千米，距省会贵阳市 240 千米，距毕节飞雄机场 80 千米，距杭瑞高速九洞天收费站 10 千米，交通便利。

The Jiudongtian National Scenic Area consists of the Zongxi River Bishui Corridor Scenic Area, the Ladder Rock Strata Mountain Range Scenic Area, and the Jiudongtian Yun Dong Tian Kai Scenic Area, with a total area of 145 square kilometers. The scenic area is easy to rcach, which is 75 kilometers away from Bijie City, 54 kilometers away from Dafang County, 60 kilometers away from Nayong County, 240 kilometers away from the provincial capital Guiyang City, 80 kilometers away from Bijie Feixiong Airport, and 10 kilometers away from the Jiudongtian toll station of Hangrui Expressway.

毕节市九洞天旅游景区集溶洞、峡谷、伏流、瀑布、天桥、天坑等景观于一身，山、水、洞等空间富于变化，体现了喀斯特地貌典型性景观特征。

九洞天 Jiudongtian

九洞天 Jiudongtian

The Jiudongtian Scenic Area in Bijie City integrates karst caves, canyons, underground streams, waterfalls, overpasses, sinkholes and other landscapes. The mountain, water, and cave in the scenic area are rich in changes, reflecting the typical landscape characteristics of karst landform.

景区岩溶资源丰富，具有很高的资源价值和市场价值。内有宽阔壮丽的溶洞、奇特神异的天坑峡谷、清澈灵秀的伏流泉瀑、形状各异的天窗景观、灵气神秘的钟乳石、纹理清晰的悬崖峭壁、底蕴深厚的文化资源，有品质极高的特级景点，景观资源多样性十分明显。

The scenic area is rich in karst formations with high resource value and market value. There are wide and magnificent karst caves, strange and supernatural sinkholes and canyons, clear and graceful springs and waterfalls, skylight landscapes with different shapes, mysterious stalactite, clear cliffs, profound cultural resources, and high-grade scenic spots with obvious diversity of landscape resources.

油杉河 Youshan River

油杉河景区位于大方县境东北部，距大方县城 58 千米，距贵阳市 198 千米，距毕节飞雄机场 64 千米。景区涉及大方县星宿、雨冲两个乡 9 个建制村部分区域，规划面积 67 平方千米，分为 8 大游览区 33 个景点。景区生物资源极为丰富，森林植被保存较好，有野生植物 1,509 种、野生动物 102 种，森林覆盖率达 84%，海拔最高为 1,910 米，最低处 890 米，平均海拔 1,400 米，年平均气温 13.6℃，空气负氧离子含量高达 6 万个 / 立方厘米。

The Youshan River Scenic Area is located in the northeast of Dafang County, 58 kilometers away from Dafang County, 198 kilometers away from Guiyang City, and 64 kilometers away from Bijie Feixiong Airport. The scenic area is divided into 8 major tourist areas and 33 scenic spots,covering parts of 9 villages in Xingxiu and Yuchong townships of Dafang County, with a planned area of 67 square kilometers. The scenic area is extremely rich in biological resources, with well preserved forest vegetation. There are 1,509 species of wild plants and 102 species of wild animals, with a forest coverage

油杉河北寨沟风光 Scenery of Beihangou of Youshan River

神秘的油杉河 Mysterious Youshan River

rate of 84%. The highest altitude is 1,910 meters, the lowest point is 890 meters, and the average altitude is 1,400 meters. The annual average temperature is 13.6 ℃ , and the air negative oxygen ion content is as high as 60,000 per cubic centimeter.

景区全境奇峰连绵，沟壑幽深，溪涧凝碧，林木蓊郁，兼山石流泉之胜，集雄奇险峻之韵，主要以奇峰、异石、秀水以及原生态的森林资源为主，是典型的喀斯特森林奇观的缩影，是户外体验、拓展训练和科普考察的好去处，亦是一座得天独厚的动植物基因库，更是一个天然的大空调、大氧吧。

The scenic area is full of magnificent and precipitous mountains, deep gullies, green streams, dense forests. It is mainly composed of strange peaks, rocks, water, and original forest resources. It is a microcosm of typical karst forest landscapes, and a good place for outdoor experience, training, and science research. It is a unique gene bank of animals and plants, and also a natural large air conditioner and oxygen bar.

贵州草海国家级自然保护区
Guizhou Caohai National Nature Reserve

草海位于乌蒙山脉腹地贵州西部威宁彝族回族苗族自治县南侧，是以保护完整的、典型的高原湿地生态系统和以黑颈鹤为代表的珍稀鸟类为主的国家级自然保护区。保护区面积 120 平方千米，湿地面积 25 平方千米，是我国面积最大的构造岩溶湖，是贵州省面积最大的高原天然淡水湖泊，被列为国家一级重要湿地，是黑颈鹤主要的越冬地之一，素有“高原明珠”“鸟的天堂”“水下森林”“物种基因库”“露天博物馆”“世界十佳观鸟胜地之一”之称，具有重大生态价值。

Caohai Lake is located in the hinterland of the Wumeng Mountains and on the south of Weining Yi, Hui, and Miao Autonomous County

中国黑颈鹤之乡——威宁草海
Weining Caohai, the hometown of Black-necked crane in China

草海鸟瞰图 Aerial view of Caohai

in the western part of Guizhou. It is a national level nature reserve for protecting a complete and typical plateau wetland ecosystem and rare birds, such as black-necked cranes. With an area of 120 square kilometers and a wetland area of 25 square kilometers, the reserve is the largest tectonic karst lake in China, the largest plateau natural fresh water lake in Guizhou Province, a national level important wetland, and one of the areas for black-necked cranes to winter. It is known as "Plateau Pearl", "Bird Paradise", "Underwater Forest", "Species Gene Bank", "Outdoor Museum", and "One of the World's Top Ten Bird Watching Resorts", which has significant ecological value.

草海因水草丰茂而得名，生物资源丰富，有生物物种 2,600 余种（其中鸟类记录 246 种）。其中，属国家 I 级保护鸟类有黑颈鹤、白肩雕等 12 种；II 级保护鸟类有灰鹤、白琵鹭、黑脸琵鹭、雀鹰、松雀鹰、草原雕、白尾鹞、游隼、灰背隼、红隼、雕鸮等

39 种。在我国为数不多的亚热带高原湿地生态系统中，其生态环境具有典型性、重要性、生物多样性、气候特殊性。

Caohai Lake is named after the abundant water grass that grows within its vicinity. It boasts a rich diversity of biological resources, with over 2,600 species documented, including 246 bird species. Among them, there are 12 species of birds under national Level I protection, including black-necked cranes and white shouldered eagles, etc; there are 39 species of birds under Level II protection, including the gray crane, white spoonbill, black faced spoonbill, sparrow eagle, sparrow eagle, grassland eagle, white tailed harrier, peregrine falcon, gray backed falcon, red falcon, and carved owl, etc. Among the few subtropical plateau wetland ecosystems in China, Caohai ecosystem has the characteristics of typicality, importance, biodiversity, and climate specificity.

民俗文化 Folk Culture

滚山珠 Gunshanzhu

滚山珠，原名“地龙滚荆”，流传于毕节苗族聚居区，以纳雍县猪场苗族彝族乡为代表。“地龙滚荆”动作古朴雅拙，贴近自然。

Gunshanzhu (Rolling Through the Thornbushes), formerly known as "Earth Dragon Rolls Through the Thorns", has been passed down in the Miao and Yi ethnic communities of Bijie, represented by the performance in the Zhuchang Miao and Yi ethnic townships of Nayong County. The movements of "Earth Dragon Rolls Through the Thorns" are simple, elegant and natural.

传说在远古时期，苗族先民在大迁徙途中，来到黑洋大箐外，前方道路坎坷，荆棘遍野，英勇的苗族青年为了给族人开辟一条

滚山珠“双飞燕” "Double Flying Swallows" in Gunshanzhu

滚山珠“叠罗汉” Stacking in Gunshanzhu

通道，就用自己矫健的身躯从荆棘中滚出一条路让族人通过，到达黑洋大箐安家落户。人们为了纪念这些年轻人的功绩，就模仿他们用身躯滚倒荆棘的动作，以舞蹈的形式记录下大迁徙的历史。

It is said that the ancestors of the Miao ethnic group came to the outside of Heiyang Daqing on their way during the Great Migration in ancient times. The road ahead was bumpy, and thorns were everywhere. In order to open up a passage for the tribe, the brave Miao youth used their strong bodies to roll out a path through the thorns. The tribe passed through successfully and settled down in Heiyang Daqing. In order to commemorate those Miao youth's contributions, people imitated their movements of rolling through the thorns and recorded the history of the Great Migration in the form of dance.

在表演中，表演者手执芦笙一边吹奏，一边跳跃，围着棱镖或水碗翻滚。在长期的演变过程中，人们逐渐将生产和生活中一些生动技巧融会到芦笙舞蹈中，不断改进完善。舞蹈动作古朴，刚柔相济，集芦笙吹奏、舞蹈表演、高难技巧艺术于一体，深受观众喜爱。

In the performance, the performer holds a lusheng (a reed-pipe wind instrument) and plays it while jumping, rolling around the darts or water bowls. In the long-term evolution process, people gradually integrated some vivid techniques from production and life into the lusheng dance, and continuously improved it. The dance movements are ancient and simple, balancing hardness with softness. It combines lusheng playing, dance performance, and acrobatics, which is very popular among the audience.

铃铛舞 Bell Dance

彝族铃铛舞俗称跳脚，彝语称“恳合呗”，是彝族在祭祀中的一种传统民间舞蹈，经过艺术处理，内容健康，风格朴实。舞者先歌后舞，歌舞相间，舞蹈无音乐伴奏，靠鼓点及舞者摇响手

彝族铃铛舞 Yi Bell Dance

中的铜铃统一动作，唢呐作间隙吹奏，以此展现彝族人民传统的生产生活场景。2008 年 6 月 7 日，彝族铃铛舞经国务院批准列入第二批国家级非物质文化遗产代表性项目名录。

The Bell Dance or "Tiaojiao", also known as "Kenhebei" in the Yi language, is a traditional folk dance performed by the Yi ethnic group during sacrificial ceremonies. It has undergone artistic refinement and embodies positive contents and simplistic style. The dancers seamlessly integrate singing and dancing, with the dance itself unaccompanied by music. Instead, the synchronized movements rely on the beats of drums and the resonating sound of copper bells held by the dancers. Occasionally, the musical instrument suona (a traditional Chinese double-reed horn) is played in the intervals. Through this dance, the traditional scenes depicting the Yi people's production and daily life are presented. On June 7, 2008, the Bell Dance was officially listed as part of the second batch of national intangible cultural heritage representative projects list with the approval of the State Council.

撮泰吉 Cuotaiji

撮泰吉，是威宁彝族回族苗族自治县板底乡裸嘎寨的一种古老的彝族戏剧。撮泰吉为彝语音译，“撮”字意为鬼，“泰”字意为变化，“吉”字意为游戏，通译为“变人戏”或“人类变化的戏”。其源于何时，至今尚无定论。

Cuotaiji is an ancient Yi drama from Luoga Village, Bandi Township, Weining Yi, Hui, and Miao Autonomous County. Cuotaiji is a transliteration of Yi language, with the word "Cuo" meaning ghost, "Tai" meaning change, and "Ji" meaning game. It is translated as "transforming people's play" or "play of human transformation". Its origins are still uncertain and remain a topic of debate.

撮泰吉 Cuotaiji

撮泰吉一般于农历正月初三到十五表演，旨在驱邪祟、迎吉祥、祈丰收。表演多在夜晚进行，表演形式十分独特，表演者用白色头帕将头缠成尖锥形，身体及四肢用布紧缠，部分人头戴面具，所戴面具主要有彝族老人、老妇人、苗族老人、汉族老人及小孩 5 种。不戴面具者为山林老人或山神，是自然与智慧的化身。

Cuotaiji is usually performed on the third to fifteenth of the first lunar month, aiming to ward off evil spirits, welcome good luck, and pray for a bountiful harvest. It is often performed at night, and the form of performance is very unique. The performers use white headscarves to wrap their heads into pointed cones, and wrap their bodies and limbs tightly with cloth. Some of them wear masks, which mainly include five faces: a Yi elderly man, an elderly woman, a Miao elderly man, a Han elderly man, and a child. Those that do not

撮泰吉 Cuotaiji

wear masks are elders in the forest or mountain gods, who are the embodiment of nature and wisdom.

撮泰吉表演主要分为祭祀、耕作、喜庆、扫寨四个部分，其中耕作是全戏的核心，主要反映彝族迁徙、农耕、繁衍的历史过程。撮泰吉是当地民众祭祀祖先，祈愿六畜兴旺、风调雨顺的重要方式，深深植根于彝族的生产、生活及文化历史中。

The performance of Cuotaiji is mainly divided into four parts: sacrificial ceremony, cultivation, celebration, and village sweeping. Among them, cultivation is the core of the entire drama, mainly reflecting the historical process of Yi people's migration, farming, and reproduction. Cuotaiji is an important way for local people to worship their ancestors and pray for the prosperity of livestock and favorable weather, which is deeply rooted in production, life, and cultural history of the Yi ethnic group.

金沙傩戏 Jinsha Nuo Opera

金沙傩戏，又叫长坝端公戏、庆坛，流传于金沙县境内。庆坛分文坛和武坛，文坛为亡人做道场，武坛即唱端公戏，文坛是忧事，武坛是喜事。该习俗在当地已流传了两百余年，传承方式主要是口传心授，属“傩及祭祀仪式性的戏曲剧种”，唱、念、做、打俱全，由开坛礼请、发碟、招兵、领牲、大开砍、收龟蛇等折子戏组成。

Jinsha Nuo Opera, also known as Changba Duangong Opera or Qingtan, has been passed down in Jinsha County. Qingtan is divided into the literary arena and the martial arts arena. The literary arena serves as religious rituals for the deceased, while the martial arts arena is known as the "Duangong Opera". The literary arena is a source of sorrow, while the martial arts arena is a source of joy. This custom has been passed down in the local area for over two hundred years, mainly through oral transmission and face to face instruction. It belongs to the "Nuo and sacrificial ritual opera genre". It involves singing, reciting, acrobatics, and fighting, and consists of several sub-performances, such as opening ceremonies, plate-throwing, recruiting soldiers, leading animals, chopping logs, and capturing turtles and snakes.

特色美食毕节菜 Delicacies in Bijie

毕节是多民族聚居的高原山区，在漫长的历史进程中，用民族特色和地域食材，形成了“酸”“辣”“香”的毕节美食风味。

Bijie is a high-altitude mountainous region with a diverse population of ethnic groups. Over the course of its rich history, the locals have developed their own unique culinary style, characterized by the use of distinct ethnic ingredients and local produce, resulting in a cuisine famous for its sour, spicy, and fragrant flavors.

毕节名菜 Famous Bijie Dishes

宫保鸡丁 Kung Pao chicken

毕节美食丰富多彩，称得上毕节名菜的主要有以下菜肴：织金宫保鸡丁、织金水八碗、竹荪乌骨鸡、脆皮竹荪、七星关酸菜肉末小豆汤、天麻药膳鸡、王傻子烧鸡、酸辣蕨粉、大方腐皮干锅鸡、骟鸡点豆腐、烙锅豆干、天麻乌鸡汤、圆子菜豆腐、里脊魔芋、黔西稻香一品酥、水西辣子鸡、金沙田园排骨、纳雍奢香火把鱼、干锅牛肉、赫章彝家坨坨肉、赫章黄帝脆玉米、赫章可乐猪、威宁火腿、威宁火腿荞饭等。

Bijie cuisine is rich and diverse. The famous dishes are the following: Zhijin Kung Pao chicken, Zhijin steamed and stewed eight

织金水八碗
Zhijin steamed and stewed eight dishes

威宁火腿
Weining Ham

dishes, bamboo fungus with black bone chicken, crisp bamboo fungus, Qixingguan pickle minced pork bean soup, Tianma chicken, Wang Shazi roast chicken, Hot and sour fern powder, Dafang toufu skin with chicken pot, Tofu with chicken, Pan-fried tofu, Tianma with black bone chicken soup, Minced-pork ball with tofu, Pork fillets with konjac, Qianxi Daoxiang Yipin crisp, Shuixi spicy chicken, Jinsha pork ribs, Nayong Shexiang grilled fish, Beef Pot, Hezhang Yi-style stewed pork, Hezhang Huangdi Crispy Corn, Hezhang Kele pork, Weining Ham, Weining Ham and Buckwheat Rice, etc.

风味小吃 Snacks

主要有毕节汤圆、康家脆哨面、刘家脆哨面、大方五香豆干、黔西化屋黄粑、金沙羊肉粉、纳雍茅香粑、赫章核桃糖、织金发粑、织金荞凉粉、赫章苦荞薄饼、威宁小粑粑、威宁牛干巴、威宁荞酥、威宁洋芋等色香味俱全的风味小吃。

毕节汤圆 Bijie rice dumpling

The local snacks mainly include Bijie rice dumpling, Kangjia crisp pork noodle, Liujia crisp pork noodle, Dafang spiced dried tofu, Qianxi Huawu Huangba, Jinsha mutton rice noodle, Nayong Mao Xiang steamed cake, Hezhang walnut candy, Zhijin steamed rice cake, Zhijin Buckwheat Jelly, Hezhang Tartary Buckwheat Pancake, Weining pan-fried dumplings, Weining beef jerky, Weining Buckwheat Crisp, Weining Potato, and so on.

地方特产 Local Specialties

茶叶 Tea

毕节地处茶树原产地区域，“高海拔、低纬度、多云雾、寡日照”的气候特点确保了茶树新梢持嫩性强，鲜叶内氨基酸、茶多酚等主要营养物质含量高，所制茶叶以“香高馥郁、鲜爽醇厚、汤色明亮、回味悠长”而闻名，特别是水浸出物含量超 40%，在全国处于一流水平。

Bijie is located in the original tea producing regions. The climate characteristics of "high altitude, low latitude, frequent cloud and fog, and rare sunlight" ensure the strong tenderness of the new tea shoots and rich nutrients such as amino acids and tea polyphenols in fresh leaves. The tea is famous for its "pleasant aroma, mellow flavor, bright color, and long aftertaste", especially the extractive values exceeding 40%, which is at the first-class level in the country.

毕节茶具有“独”“特”“优”三个特点。独：毕节茶生长于高海拔地区，拥有独具特色的生态环境。特：高海拔茶园日夜温差大，使得毕节茶的芳香物质更加丰富，具有特殊的香气。优：毕节茶品质好、口味好、汤色好，夏秋茶可比江浙一带春茶。三者俱备，国内外少有，彰显毕节茶的综合优势，具有独特吸引力和竞争力，发展前景好。

采收茶叶 Harvesting tea leaves

纳雍县高山生态茶园
Ecological Tea Gardens in mountain region in Nayong County

Bijie tea is distinguished by three unique characteristics: "uniqueness", "specialty", and "superiority". The term "uniqueness" refers to the fact that Bijie tea is grown in high-altitude regions, possessing a distinctive ecological environment. "Specialty" indicates that the significant temperature fluctuations in high-altitude tea gardens result in a richer concentration of aromatic compounds in the tea leaves, giving Bijie tea its unique fragrance. Finally, "superiority" signifies the excellent quality, taste, and color of Bijie tea, which can rival spring tea grown in Zhejiang and Jiangsu provinces. These three features are rare both domestically and internationally, highlighting the comprehensive advantages of Bijie tea and making it highly attractive and competitive with great potential for development.

天麻 Tianma (Gastrodia elata)

毕节市位于乌蒙山腹地，森林密布，气候温润，土壤富含微量元素，是天麻生长的天堂，是贵州乃至全国重要的天麻产区。毕节天麻外形饱满、肉质肥厚、浆汁丰富、绿色生态、入口回甘，是国内外公认质量较好的地道药材。

Bijie City is situated in the heartland of the Wumeng Mountains, boasting dense forests, a temperate climate, and soil that is abundant in trace elements. It is an ideal environment for the cultivation of gastrodia elata, and a significant production hub for this precious herb in Guizhou as well as the entire country. The gastrodia elata grown in Bijie has a full-bodied appearance, thick flesh, rich juice, green ecology, and leaves a sweet aftertaste upon consumption. It is widely recognized both domestically and internationally as a high-quality and authentic Chinese medicinal herb.

毕节天麻 Bijie Tianma

大方天麻
Dafang Tianma

天麻加工
Tianma processing

全市有 30 家天麻规模加工企业。其中 4 家加工龙头企业，年产能约 1,000 吨，产品有天麻饮片、天麻胶囊、天麻酒、鲜天麻冻干粉、保鲜天麻、食得乐颗粒、天麻饮料、天麻蜜饯、天麻茶等天麻系列产品。

There are 30 large-scale gastrodia elata processing enterprises in the city. Among them, there are four leading processing enterprises with an annual production capacity of approximately 1,000 tons. The products include gastrodia elata decoction pieces, capsules, liquor, freeze-dried powder, fresh gastrodia elata, granules, beverage, preserves, tea, and other series products.

毕节市天麻主要采取“短材小窝塘”（先培菌材后放麻种）和“大菌棒种植”林下仿野生的生态种植模式，按照“人种天养”的管理方法，还原天麻“原生态”特性，培育高品质天麻。

Bijie City mainly employs two ecological planting methods, namely "cultivating spawn using short materials in small ponds" and "planting large mushroom sticks" in the forest understory to cultivate gastrodia elata. By adhering to the management principle of "human plant while nature cultivate", it effectively restores the natural ecology of gastrodia elata, resulting in high-quality yields.

食用菌 Edible Mushrooms

2022 年，全市种植食用菌 13.79 万亩、产量 41.1 万吨、产值 65 亿元，产业规模居全省第一位。

In 2022, the city planted 137,900 acres of edible mushrooms, with a yield of 411,000 tons and an output value of 6.5 billion yuan, ranking first in the province in terms of industrial scale.

近年来，毕节市加快农业强市建设，围绕发展食用菌战略部署，培育了市级以上龙头企业 30 家（国家级 1 家、省级 12 家），打造了“织金竹荪”“金荪生物”等一批竞争力较强、名誉度较高的食用菌品牌。全市先后建成了大方县中国白参科创园、织金县“国家竹荪种植标准化示范区”、黔西市香菇标准化种植示范区、威宁彝族回族苗族自治县食用菌产业基地，推动产业标准化生产。

在绿塘乡龙昌坪冬荪基地，冬荪长势喜人

Dongsun in Longchangping Dongsun Base, Lvtang Township

织金竹荪 Zhijin bamboo fungus

In recent years, Bijie has accelerated the development of a competitive city in agriculture, prioritizing the development of the edible mushrooms. Because of this strategy, 30 leading enterprises have emerged, including one at the national level and 12 at provincial level. creating a group of highly competitive and reputable edible mushrooms brands such as "Zhijin Bamboo Fungus" and "Jinsun Biological". The city has successively established the China Baishen Science and Technology Innovation Park in Dafang County, the "National Bamboo Fungus Planting Standardization Demonstration Zone" in Zhijin County, the Standardized Mushroom Planting Demonstration Zone in Qianxi City, and the Edible Mushrooms Industry Base in Weining Yi, Hui, and Miao Autonomous County, promoting industrial standardization production.

古迹遗址 Relics and Sites

赫章县可乐遗址 Hezhang Kele Site

可乐遗址位于贵州省赫章县城西北约 60 千米处的可乐乡，地处黔西北乌蒙山脉中段。遗址区为一山间谷地，乌江北源支流可乐河、麻腮河于坝中交汇，坝子四周多缓坡丘陵，向外群山环拱。可乐遗址总面积约 9.4 平方千米，在众多的缓坡台地上，分布着大量战国至秦汉时期的遗存。类型包括聚落遗址 2 处，手工业遗址 1 处，墓葬遗址 15 处。

The Kele Site is situated in Kele Township, about 60 kilometers northwest of Hezhang County in Guizhou Province, within the middle section of the Wumeng Mountains in northwest Guizhou. Covering a valley within the mountains, the site is located in the middle of a dam where Kele River and Masai River converge, surrounded by gentle slopes and hills that are enclosed by mountains. The Kele Site covers

可乐遗址全景 Panorama of the Kele Site

可乐夜郎时期墓地发掘现场
The excavation of the cemetery during the Yelang period in the Kele Site

an area of approximately 9.4 square kilometers and contains relics from the Warring States period to the Qin and Han dynasties . These artifacts are scattered throughout many gently sloping terraces. Among the collection of relics, there are two settlement sites, one handcraft industry site, and 15 tombs.

这些遗址（墓群）被天然的河流划分为可乐河南区、麻腮河西区、乡政府北区三个区，其中乡政府北区和麻腮河西区各有一个居住遗址，居址旁边另有墓地分布。

Thc Kele Site's tombs are divided into three areas by the river: the southern Kele River area, the western Masai River area, and the northern township government area. There is one residential site and an adjacent cemetery in both the western Masai River area and the northern township government area.

1960 年至 2012 年，考古单位在可乐遗址（墓群）共进行 10 次考古发掘，其中，2000 年至 2001 年的考古发掘入选“2001 年全国十大考古新发现”。

From 1960 to 2012, archaeological units conducted a total of ten excavations at the Kele Site. The excavation in 2000-2001 was recognized as one of China's top ten archaeological discoveries in 2001.

可乐遗址出土的铜柄铁短剑
An iron short sword with bronze hilt unearthed from the Kele Site

1982 年，贵州省人民政府公布可乐遗址（墓群）为省级文物保护单位。2001 年，国务院公布其为全国重点文物保护单位。

The Kele Site was declared a provincial-level cultural relic protection unit by the People's Government of Guizhou Province in 1982. Later, in 2001, it was declared a Key National Cultural Relic Protection Unit by the State Council.

黔西观音洞遗址 Qianxi Guanyindong Site

黔西观音洞遗址位于黔西市观音洞镇观音洞村，距城 30 千米，东经 105° 57′，北纬 26° 51′。其洞系石灰岩构成，高出洼地 15 米，分为主洞和南北两个支洞，主洞长 9 米，宽 2—4 米，支洞长 5 米，宽 1—2 米。洞穴堆积厚达 9 米，分上、下两部分，延续时代距今 24 万年至 4 万年。黔西观音洞遗址是我国长江以南发现的第一处旧石器时代早期最大的遗址。

Located in Guanyindong Village, Guanyindong Town, and with coordinates of 105°57'E and 26°51'N, the Guanyindong Site is a limestone cave situated approximately 30 kilometers from Qianxi City. It rises 15 meters above the surrounding depression and comprises a main cave and two supporting caves to the north and south. The main

科研人员正在考察黔西观音洞遗址内部
Researchers inspecting the interior of Qianxi Guanyindong Site

cave measures 9 meters in length and 2-4 meters in width, while the supporting caves are 5 meters long and 1-2 meters wide. The cave has a sediment thickness of 9 meters, which can be divided into upper and lower layers that span from around 240,000 years ago to 40,000 years ago. The Guanyindong Site is the largest Paleolithic site discovered to date south of the Yangtze River in China.

1958 年，人们发现观音洞遗址。1964 年至 1973 年，中国科学院古脊椎动物与古人类研究所、贵州省博物馆、贵州省科学院等单位先后对观音洞进行 4 次发掘，共出土石制品 4,000 多件，以及东方剑齿象为主的 23 种哺乳动物化石，其中石制品有砍砸器、刮削器、端尖器、雕刻器、尖状器等，其大部分特征为其他地方所没有，反映了西南地区旧石器时代文化发展的特点，被命名为黔西“观音洞文化”。

The Guanyindong Site was first discovered in 1958, and subsequently excavated by the Institute of Vertebrate Paleontology and Paleoanthropology of the Chinese Academy of Sciences, the Guizhou Provincial Museum, the Guizhou Academy of Sciences, and other organizations between 1964 and 1973. Over 4,000 stone artifacts and 23 types of mammalian fossils were unearthed during these excavations, with Oriental elephants being the most common. The stone artifacts included chopping tools, scraping tools, pointed tools, carving tools, and pointed implements, many of which had unique characteristics not found anywhere else. These discoveries offer insight into the development of Paleolithic culture in Southwest China and have been named the "Guanyindong Culture" of Qianxi.

2018 年 11 月 20 日，《自然》杂志发表研究文章指出，距今 17 万年至 8 万年前，贵州省黔西县（现为黔西市）观音洞遗址出现了勒瓦娄哇技术。黔西观音洞遗址勒瓦娄哇技术的重大发现，提供了东亚古人类在中晚更新世拥有预制石核技术的可靠证据，更新了关于东亚古人类技术发展水平的认识，丰富了关于古人类在东亚的交流进化历史。1982 年 2 月 23 日，观音洞遗址获批为省级文物保护单位；2001 年 6 月 25 日，观音洞遗址获批为全国重点文物保护单位。

黔西观音洞遗址动物化石
Animal fossils unearthed from Qianxi Guanyindong Site

黔西观音洞遗址出土石制品
Stone products unearthed from Qianxi Guanyindong Site

An article published in *Nature* on November 20, 2018 reported the discovery of Levallois technology at the Guanyindong Site in Qianxi County, Guizhou Province, dating back to approximately 170,000 to 80,000 years ago. This groundbreaking discovery provides strong evidence that ancient humans in East Asia utilized pre-prepared stone core technology during the middle and late Pleistocene epoch, contributing significantly to better understanding of their technological development and enriching our knowledge of their evolutionary history. The Guanyindong Site was granted Provincial Cultural Relic Protection Unit on February 23, 1982, and declared a Key National Cultural Relic Protection Unit on June 25, 2001.

威宁中水遗址 Weining Zhongshui Site

中水遗址位于威宁彝族回族苗族自治县中水镇小盆地内，总面积约 5 万平方米。2004 年至 2005 年，贵州省文物考古研究所在中水的鸡公山进行了两次发掘，发掘点都位于中水盆地内中河两侧的坡地和山梁上，揭露面积近 3,000 平方米，清理出祭坑、墓葬、灰坑、房址、沟等 200 余处，出土近 1,000 件陶器、石器、骨器、玉石器、青铜器等文化遗物，获得了重大成果。据考证，中水遗址群的时代早期处于新石器时代末期，晚期已进入青铜器时代，相当于中原商周之际，距今 3,500 年至 2,700 年。

Zhongshui Site is located in the basin of Zhongshui Town, Weining Yi, Hui, and Miao Autonomous County. This site encompasses an area of roughly 50,000 square meters and was excavated twice in Jigong Mountain by the Guizhou Provincial Institute of Cultural Relics and Archaeology from 2004 to 2005. The excavation site spanned nearly 3,000 square meters on the slopes and ridges on both sides of the Zhonghe River in the Zhongshui Basin. Over 200 sacrificial pits, tombs, ash pits, house sites, ditches, and other artifacts were uncovered during excavation, with almost 1,000 cultural relics discovered, including pottery, stone tools, bone tools, jade tools, and bronze ware. These discoveries provide important insights into the region's history. Research indicates that the Zhongshui Site dates back to the late Neolithic period and transitions into the Bronze Age, similar to the Shang and Zhou dynasties in the Central Plains, with a history dating back approximately 3,500-2,700 years ago.

遗址中发现大量水稻标本，80% 以上的遗址坑都有水稻颗粒出土。这是在西南地区发现的最早旱稻农业的实物遗存。

A large number of rice specimens were discovered at the site, with more than 80% of the pit's artifacts containing rice grains, making it the earliest known physical evidence of dry rice agriculture discovered in southwest China.

中水遗址 Zhongshui Site

2005 年，中水遗址被评为“全国十大考古新发现”。2006 年，被列为省级文物保护单位。

In 2005, Zhongshui Site was included among the "Top Ten New Archaeological Discoveries in China", and was designated as a provincial-level cultural relic protection unit in 2006.

贵州宣慰府 Guizhou Xuanweifu

贵州宣慰府坐落于慕俄格古城中。慕俄格古城是古罗甸王国的首府。“慕俄格”是彝语，意为天下彝族君王居住的地方，后逐渐成为地名，现为大方县城所在地。

The Guizhou Xuanweifu is located in Muege Old Town. The Muege Old Town was the capital of the ancient Luodian Kingdom. The name "Muege" originated from the Yi language and means the place where Yi kings reside. Gradually, it became the name of the location that is now known as Dafang County.

贵州宣慰府 Guizhou Xuanweifu

贵州宣慰府全景俯拍
Panoramic aerial view of Guizhou Xuanweifu

慕俄格古城始建于蜀汉时期，唐时修建了宏伟的九重宫殿，宋时改封为罗施国，赐首领为“罗施鬼主”，元置顺元宣慰司，明置贵州宣慰司。

The Muege Old Town has a long history, originally established during the Shu Han period and expanded into a grand nine-story palace during the Tang Dynasty. In the Song Dynasty, it was known as Luoshiguo and the leader was given the title of "Luoshigui Master". During the Yuan Dynasty, it was transformed into the Shunyuan Xuanweisi, and in the Ming Dynasty, it was renamed the Guizhou Xuanweisi.

恢复重建的贵州宣慰府共“一场八院九层”，规划面积 4.56 平方千米，占地 300 多亩，是大型电视连续剧《奢香夫人》的取景地。2012 年 8 月 20 日，慕俄格古城被中国广播电视协会、电视制片人协会评为全国影视指定拍摄地。古城处于海拔 1,650 米至 2,000 米，年平均气温 11 ℃，是理想的休闲避暑旅游目的地。

Guizhou Xuanweifu has been reconstructed, including one courtyard, eight halls, and nine floors. Its planned area is 4.56 square kilometers. Now it covers over 300 mu (approximately 20 hectares) of land. Guizhou Xuanweifu is the filming site for the grand TV series "*Madame Shexiang*". On August 20th, 2012, the Muege Old Town was recognized by the China Television Artists Association and Television Producers Association as a designated national film and television shooting location. The old town is located at an altitude of 1,650 to 2,000 meters with an average annual temperature of 11℃ , making it an ideal destination for leisure and summer vacations.

电视剧《奢香夫人》先后被评为第九届全国十佳优秀电视剧、第二十六届中国电视金鹰节优秀电视剧奖和最佳美术奖、第十二届精神文明建设“五个一工程”奖。

The TV series "*Madame Shexiang*" has been recognized with multiple awards. Notably, it won the Top Ten Outstanding TV Series at the Ninth National Television Awards, as well as the Excellent TV Drama Award and Best Artistic Design Award at the 26th China TV Golden Eagle Award. The series also received the Five-One Project Award for the Twelfth Spiritual Civilization Construction.

大屯土司庄园 Datun Tusi Manor

大屯土司庄园位于毕节市东北 108 千米的大屯彝族乡大屯村，系彝族土司余像仪建于清道光年间。其依山势而建，梯级渐升，后经其子余若瑔扩建。大屯土司庄园占地约 5,000 平方米，建筑面积 2,600 平方米，坐东南向西北，三组平行三进梯级上升院落。中轴线为大堂、二堂、正堂，大堂面阔五间，进深四间，穿斗式梁架，屋顶左为封火山墙，右为歇山。北轴线为花园、客房、粮仓、绣楼。客房面阔五间，进深二间，穿斗式硬山墙青瓦顶，南轴线为轿厅、愫雅堂、廊桥、鱼池、宗祠、厨房等。愫雅堂面阔三间，穿斗式歇山青瓦顶，四周有回廊。门楼一座，碉堡六座。大屯土司庄园为全国保存最为完好的彝族土司庄园之一，是研究彝族建筑艺术、历史文化等具有代表性的实物史料。1988 年，国务院将其公布为全国重点文物保护单位。

Datun Tusi Manor is situated in Datun Village, Datun Yi Autonomous Township, which is located 108 kilometers northeast of Bijie City. It was constructed during the reign of Emperor Daoguang of the Qing Dynasty by Tusi Yu Xiangyi of the Yi ethnic group. The manor was built according to the mountain's natural terrain, with levels that gradually ascend, and was later expanded by Yu Ruoquan. Covering an area of over 5,000 square meters, the Datun Tusi Manor has a building area of 2,600 square meters. It is oriented towards the southeast and

大屯土司庄园 Datun Tusi Manor

northwest and consists of three parallel and rising courtyards with the main hall, second hall, and main hall on the central axis. The main hall is five bays wide and four bays deep, featuring a crossed-beam roof structure. The roof's left side is a wall with enclosed fire prevention function, and the right side is a gable roof. The northern axis includes a garden, guest rooms, granaries, and embroidery buildings. The guest rooms are five bays wide and two bays deep, with a crossed-beam hard mountain wall and a blue tile roof. The southern axis comprises a sedan hall, Suiya hall, gallery bridge, fish pond, ancestral temple, and kitchen. The Suiya Hall is three bays wide, with a crossed-beam gable roof and a surrounding corridor. In addition, there is one gatehouse and six watchtowers. Datun Tusi Manor is one of the most well-preserved Yi Tusi manors in China and an invaluable material evidence for studying architecture, art, history, and culture of the Yi ethnic group. In 1988, it was recognized as a national key cultural relics protection unit by the State Council.

黔西象祠 Qianxi Xiang Temple

黔西象祠遗址位于贵州省黔西市素朴镇灵博社区九龙山，东经106°20.628′，北纬 26°59.588′。其始建于隋末。象祠是祭祀象的寺庙，传说象是舜同父异母的兄弟，初时不仁，多次设计害舜，欲夺其位，霸其妻及财产。舜不予计较，常以德感化象，终于使象弃恶从善，勤于政务，泽加于民。此后，人们为怀念他而建寺庙供奉。

Qianxi Xiang Temple is located in the Jiulongshan area of Lingbo Community, Supu Town, Qianxi City, Guizhou Province. Its precise coordinates are 106°20.628' east longitude and 26°59.588' north latitude. Founded in the late Sui Dynasty, this temple is dedicated to the worship of Xiang. According to legend, Xiang is the half-brother of Shun, who once plotted against him and coveted his position and property. However, Shun's unwavering virtue ultimately influenced Xiang to turn away from evil and become a diligent political figure who worked for the benefit of the people. Since then, people have built temples in honor of him.

明正德三年（1508 年），贵州宣慰使（水西土司）安贵荣翻修象祠时请当时被贬到修文龙场做驿丞的王阳明为之作记。《象祠记》被收入《古文观止》，成为不朽的名篇。建筑依山而建，就山势而布局，毁于吴三桂平定水西时的战火，后又增建四进四重的宏大佛教建筑，分别有山关殿、大佛殿、观音殿、文昌阁、禅房等。现残存清代所建禅房一间，碑刻两通，基石无数，石坝子、石坎等若干。

象祠 Xiang Temple

象祠之一堂两馆 Halls of the Xiang Temple

During the third year of Emperor Zhengde's reign in the Ming Dynasty (1508), An Guirong, the Governor of Guizhou Province (Shuixi Tusi), oversaw the rebuilding of the Xiang Temple and invited Wang Yangming, who had been demoted to Xiuwen Longchang as a postmaster at the time, to document the process. The resulting work, titled "*Record of the Xiang Temple*", was included in the "*Guwen Guanzhi*" and is considered an immortal masterpiece. Unfortunately, the temple was destroyed during the war when Wu Sangui pacified Shuixi. Later on, it was rebuilt and expanded to include four sets of grand Buddhist buildings, including the Shanguan Hall, Great Buddha Hall, Avalokitesvara Hall, Wenchang Pavilion, and Mediation Room. Although only one Mediation room constructed during the Qing Dynasty remains today, there are two inscriptions as well as numerous foundation stones, stone dams, and stone ridges on the site.

黔西象祠遗址现为中国仅存的象祠遗址，对于研究古代水西土司制度、军事、政治、边疆、民族以及中国古典哲学、中国古代文化、中国古代民俗等具有非常重要、不可替代的作用。

As the only remaining Xiang Temple in China, the Qianxi Xiang Temple plays an essential and irreplaceable role in studying ancient systems of Shuixi Tusi, military, politics, border areas, ethnic groups, as well as Chinese classical philosophy, ancient culture, and folk customs.

1996 年 5 月，象祠被列为县级文物保护单位；2015 年 5 月，象祠被列为省级文物保护单位。

In May 1996, the Xiang Temple was listed as a county-level cultural relic protection unit, while in May 2015, it was upgraded to be a provincial-level cultural relic protection unit.

奢香博物馆 Shexiang Museum

奢香博物馆位于贵州省大方县城北云龙山脚洗马塘畔。奢香博物馆以明代摄贵州宣慰使“明顺德夫人”奢香命名，与奢香墓共建在同一保护范围内。奢香博物馆具有鲜明的古代彝族土司庄园的传统建筑艺术风格，从布局到结构遵循了黔西北彝族古代土司建筑依山顺势梯建的双重四合院落风格，整个建筑融入了彝族崇龙尚虎的艺术元素。

奢香夫人铜像
Bronze Statue of Madame Shexiang

Shexiang Museum is situated near the Xima Pond at the foot of Yunlong Mountain in the northern region of Dafang County, Guizhou Province. It takes its name from Shexiang, an imperial envoy to Guizhou during the Ming Dynasty, who is buried within the same protected area as the museum. The museum's architectural style reflects the traditional estates of ancient Yi ethnic chieftains in northwestern Guizhou, featuring a unique double courtyard design that conforms to the hillside terrain and incorporates artistic elements representing the Yi people's reverence for dragons and tigers.

老馆于 1993 年 3 月破土动工，1994 年 4 月竣工并对外开放。2009 年，奢香博物馆进行提质升级建设，改造“奢香专题馆”，建设“彝族历史文化综合馆”，建成后的“奢香专题馆”和“彝族历史文化综合馆”总占地面积为36,865平方米，建筑面积为3,800余平方米，展厅面积为2,800平方米。博物馆以“彝族珍粹”与“人民智慧”两部分为基本陈列，设“奢香专题馆”和“彝族历史文化综合馆”及临展区，馆内共收藏彝族文物藏品1,400余件。

The groundbreaking for the Old Building occurred in March 1993, and it was completed and opened to the public in April 1994. Later, in 2009, the museum underwent a substantial upgrade and renovation, which included the transformation of the "Shexiang Special Museum" and the construction of the "Yi Ethnic History and Culture Complex Museum". Today, the entire museum complex covers a total area of 36,865 square meters, with a built-up area exceeding 3,800 square meters, as well as an exhibition space of 2,800 square meters dedicated to showcasing over 1,400 pieces of Yi ethnic cultural relics. The museum's exhibits are primarily divided into two sections: "The

奢香博物馆 Shexiang Museum

Essence of Yi Ethnic Culture" and "People's Wisdom", with a "She Xiang Thematic Hall", a "Yi History and Culture Comprehensive Hall" as well as a temporary exhibition area.

奢香博物馆先后获评为“贵州省爱国主义教育基地”“全国民族团结进步教育基地”“全国文物系统先进集体”“国家三级博物馆”等，年平均接待参观达 30 万人次。

The Shexiang Museum has gained recognition as a "Patriotic Education Base in Guizhou Province", "National Unity and Progress Education Base", "National Advanced Cultural Relics System Collective", and a "National Level-3 Museum". With an annual average of 300,000 visitors.

美丽乡村 Beautiful Countryside

化屋村 Huawu Village

2021 年 2 月 3 日，习近平总书记视察贵州，第一站就来到化屋村，亲切看望各族干部群众。

On February 3, 2021, General Secretary of CPC Central Committe Xi Jinping paid a visit to Guizhou. His first destination was Huawu Village, where he cordially met officials and people of all ethnic groups there.

黔西市新仁苗族乡化屋村位于百里乌江画廊鸭池河大峡谷、东风湖北岸。全村居住有苗族、彝族、汉族，辖 3 个村民组 284 户 1,133 人，其中苗族 275 户 1,096 人，占比 96.7%。

Huawu village in Xinren Miao Ethnic Township is located in Baili Gallery of wujiang River source, Yachi River Grand Canyon, and on the

化屋码头 Huawu Wharf

northern shore of Dongfeng Lake in Qianxi City. The village is home to Miao, Yi, and Han ethnic groups and consists of three village groups with a total of 284 households and 1,133 residents. 275 households and 1,096 individuals are of Miao ethnicity, accounting for 96.7% of the population.

化屋村民族民间文化底蕴浓厚，有拦门酒、跳花坡、篝火舞等民俗。“化屋苗族文化空间”入选贵州省第二批省级非物质文化遗产代表作名录。

Huawu Village boasts a thriving ethnic folk culture, including customs like "Lanmen Wine", "Jumping Flower Slope", and "Bonfire Dance". The "Huawu Miao Cultural Space" was selected as part of the second batch of provincial-level representative works of intangible cultural heritage in Guizhou province.

党的十八大以来，化屋村借助资源优势，推进乡村发展进入快车道，乡村建设、产业发展、村民生活水平等诸多方面都有了

黔西市新仁苗族乡易地扶贫搬迁安置化屋点
Huawu relocation sites for poverty alleviation in Xinren Miao Township, Qianxi City

新的变化。先后荣获“全省脱贫攻坚先进党组织”“全省先进基层党组织”“全国先进基层党组织”“全国乡村旅游重点村”“中国美丽休闲乡村”“全国乡村治理示范村”。

Since the 18th National Congress of the Communist Party of China, Huawu Village has capitalized on its resources and achieved rapid rural development. Many aspects of the village, including rural construction, industrial development, and the living standards of villagers, have undergone significant changes. As a result, the village has received numerous accolades, such as "Advanced Party Organization for Poverty Alleviation in the Province", "Advanced Grassroots Party Organization in the Province", "National Advanced Grassroots Party Organization", "Key Village for Rural Tourism in

海雀万亩林场 Haique Wanmu Forest Farm

China", "Beautiful and Leisurely Rural Area of China", and "National Demonstration Village for Rural Governance".

海雀村 Haique Village

海雀是毕节试验区的“发祥地”，也是“时代楷模”、全国优秀共产党员、最美奋斗者文朝荣工作和生活的地方。

Haique Village is the "cradle" of Bijie Pilot Zone. This place also gave birth to a famous excellent figure, Wen Chaorong who was awarded the various honors like the "Role Model of the Times", "The National Distinguished Member of the Communist Party", and "Role Model of Dedication".

海雀村位于赫章县河镇彝族苗族乡东北部，距乡政府所在地 12 千米，距县城所在地 110 千米，海拔 2,300 米。全村总面积 11.87 平方千米，耕地面积 1,780 亩，林地面积 13,700 亩。共辖 5 个村民组，户籍人口 228 户 1,004 人。2022 年，全村人均可支配收入 18,633 元。

Haique Village is situated in the northeast of He Township, a Yi and Miao Ethnic Township in Hezhang County. The village is located

松林环绕的海雀村
Haique Village surrounded by pine trees

12 kilometers away from the township government and 110 kilometers away from the county seat, at an altitude of 2,300 meters. The total area of the village covers 11.87 square kilometers, including 1,780 mu of arable land and 13,700 mu of forest land. It consists of five villagers' groups and has a registered population of 228 households and 1,004 individuals. In 2022, the per capita disposable income of the entire village reached 18,633 yuan.

毕节概览
2022

07

发展战略

Developmental Strategies

站在新的历史起点上，毕节全市干部群众深入贯彻习近平总书记对毕节试验区工作的重要指示精神，大力实施《推动毕节高质量发展规划》，按照省委、省政府工作部署，推动构建以建设贯彻新发展理念示范区为总体目标，以打造“两区一典范一基地”为重点任务，以政策、资源、人口“三大优势”为基础支撑，以“市场换产业、资源换投资”为重要路径，以围绕“四新”主攻“四化”为重大抓手，以实施“党建五项行动”为重要保障的高质量发展新格局，奋力谱写中国式现代化建设的毕节篇章！

At a new historical starting point, the governmental officials and the local people of Bijie City are wholeheartedly implementing the significant instructions of General Secretary Xi Jinping on the work of the Bijie Pilot Zone. They are vigorously carrying out the "*Plan to Promote High-quality Development in Bijie*" in line with the instructions of the Provincial Party Committee and Provincial Government. Their goal is to establish a model zone that embodies the construction and implementation of the new development philosophy, with a key focus on creating two zones, one model, and

推动毕节高质量发展专家指导组成立大会在北京召开
The establishiment of expert panel for high-quality development of Bijie in Beijing

毕节市党建引领基层治理和发展工作推进会暨诉源治理现场观摩会
Party building conference in Bijie

one base. This endeavor is supported by the three major advantages of policies, resources, and population. It follows the strategic approach of exchanging industries through market mechanisms and attracting investments through resource exchanges. Concentrating on "Four-pronged New Vision" (treading new paths, opening up new prospects, seizing new opportunities, and making new achievements), Bijie City will prioritize the development strategy of the Four-front Development Initiative, namely promoting new industrialization, new urbanization, agricultural modernization, and tourism industry. With the invaluable support of implementing the "Five Actions for Party Building", the aim is to achieve high-quality development and strive to write a chapter of Bijie's contribution to China's path to modernization.

建设乡村振兴新典范。毕节市将持续巩固拓展脱贫攻坚成果，全面实施乡村振兴战略，着力推进基层党建示范引领、山地高效农业突破、农村脱贫人口增收、人居环境整治、乡村“五治”融合等五项行动，统筹推进乡村“五大振兴”，实现乡村生态美环

大方县恒大幸福二村及配套蔬菜产业基地
Hengda Xingfu Second Village and Vegetable Industry Base in Dafang County

境优、生产美产业强、生活美百姓富目标，探索形成脱贫地区全面推进乡村振兴的毕节模式，建成脱贫地区乡村振兴新典范。

Constucting a new model for rural revitalization, Bijie City will continue to consolidate and expand the achievements of poverty alleviation, fully implement the strategy for rural revitalization, and prioritize five key actions including demonstration leading of grassroots party building, efficient agriculture breakthroughs in mountainous areas, income improvement for rural poor, improvement of living environments, and integration of "five rural governances". The comprehensive promotion of the "Five Revitalizations" of the

countryside will be coordinated to achieve a beautiful ecological environment, strong industries, and prosperous livelihoods for people in rural areas. Bijie City will develop and explore the Bijie model for comprehensive promotion of rural revitalization in poverty-stricken regions, aiming to build a new exemplary model for rural revitalization in these areas.

建设绿色发展样板区。毕节市将牢固树立和践行“绿水青山就是金山银山”的理念，充分考虑岩溶山区生态环境容量和资源承载力，加快新旧动能转换，逐步摆脱资源依赖，筑牢长江、珠江上游生态安全屏障，大力发展生态友好型产业，探索欠发达地区绿水青山向金山银山转换的有效路径，进一步完善绿色发展政策制度体系，为把毕节建设成为百姓富、生态美、活力强的示范区提供坚实绿色保障。

Constructing a model zone for green development, Bijie City is committed to uphold and act on the principle that lucid waters and lush mountains are invaluable assets. With careful consideration of the ecological carrying capacity and resource constraints in the karst mountainous areas, the city will expedite the transition from old to new driving forces, gradually reduce dependency on natural resources, and fortify the ecological security

金沙县后山古镇全景
Panorama of Houshan Ancient Town in Jinsha County

barrier along the Yangtze River and the upper reaches of the Pearl River. Emphasis will be placed on the robust development of eco-friendly industries, exploring effective pathways to transform the ecological beauty of underdeveloped regions into economic prosperity. Furthermore, efforts will be made to enhance the policy and institutional framework for green development. These endeavors aim to solidify a green guarantee, making Bijie City a model zone characterized with its prosperity of the residents, environmental splendor, and vibrant vitality.

建设人力资源开发培育基地。毕节市将大力实施职业教育攻坚、职业技能提升、“智慧毕节”、人才强企培育、乡村人才振兴、

人口素质提升“六项行动”，打造党政人才培育、职业教育、技能人才培育、人力资源服务、教育医疗服务“五类平台”，培育毕节鲁班、毕节织工、毕节乡厨、毕节康护、毕节农技“五大品牌”。推动人口优势转化为人口红利，实现人力资源开发工作与经济社会发展相融互促，协调发展，努力建成西部地区重要的人力资源开发培育基地。

Constructing a base for human resources development and cultivation, Bijie City is committed to make breakthroughs six aspects: vocational education, skill enhancement, the development of "Smart Bijie" , fostering talented individuals to strengthen enterprises, revitalizing rural talent, and improving population quality. The city aims to establish five platforms: talent cultivation for the Party and government, vocational education, skill training, human resources services, and education and healthcare services. It will foster five major brands: Luban craftsmen, Bijie weavers, rural chefs, healthcare

毕节职业技术学院“广州港班”学生到广州就业
Students from "Guangzhou Port Class" of Bijie Vocational and Technical College employed in Guangzhou

providers, and agricultural technicians. With the aim to promote the transition of population advantage into demographic dividend, Bijie will realize the integration, promotion and coordination of human resources development with economic and social development. The city aims to become a vital hub for human resource development and cultivation in the western region of China.

建设体制机制创新先行区。毕节市将进一步解放思想、开拓创新，强化各类改革创新举措系统集成，全面优化制度环境、强化制度供给，增强高质量发展内生动力，推动巩固拓展脱贫攻坚成果同乡村振兴有效衔接，在绿色发展、人力资源开发等重点领域率先实现改革突破，加快完善共建共享体制机制，深化拓展统一战线服务地方改革发展实践。

Constructing a pilot zone for institutional innovation, Bijie City will continue to emancipate minds, explore and innovate. It will strengthen the systematic integration of various reform and innovation measures, comprehensively optimize the institutional environment, strengthen the institutional supply, enhance the internal driving force of high-quality development, and promote the consolidation and expansion of poverty alleviation achievements with the effective connection of rural revitalization. Bijie will also take the lead in achieving reform breakthroughs in key areas such as green development and human resources development, accelerate the improvement in the system and mechanism of co-construction and sharing, deepen and expand the united front to serve local reform and development.